James Dean

BEHIND THE SCENE

James Dean

BEHIND THE SCENE

EDITED BY LEITH ADAMS AND KEITH BURNS

DESIGNED BY PAULA SCHER AND RON LOUIE

CITADEL PRESS
KENSINGTON PUBLISHING CORP.
WWW.KENSINGTONBOOKS.COM

CITADEL PRESS books are published by

Kensington Publishing Corp.
850 Third Avenue
New York, NY 10022

All Kensington titles, imprints, and distributed lines are available at special quantity discounts for bulk purchases for sales promotions, premiums, fund raising, educational, or institutional use. Special book excerpts or customized printings can also be created to fit specific needs. For details, write or phone the office of the Kensington special sales manager: Kensington Publishing Corp., 850 Third Avenue, New York, NY 10022, attn: Special Sales Department, phone 1-800-221-2647.

Citadel Press and the Citadel logo are trademarks of Kensington Publishing Corp.

First printing June 2001

10 9 8 7 6 5 4 3 2 1

Printed in the United States of America

Cataloging information is available from the Library of Congress

ISBN 0-8065-2325-5

DEDICATION

TO JAMES DEAN . . . STAR

TO JACK L. WARNER, ELIA KAZAN, NICHOLAS RAY

AND GEORGE STEVENS . . . STARMAKERS

FOREWORD

The photographs in this book are reproduced from the original negatives housed in the Warner Bros. Archives at the University of Southern California's School of Cinema-Television. Of the thousands of still photographs taken of Dean during the making of his three starring films, only a limited number were printed and used by the studio for publicity and advertising purposes. The rest lay undisturbed for over three decades until the importance of these images was discovered. But as important as these photographs are, they are made more so by the inclusion of the day-to-day production documents that accompany them.

This book is presented chronologically—film-by-film: *East of Eden*, *Rebel Without a Cause*, and *Giant*. The documents for each film are arranged by relevance, while the photos are arranged as the scenes they represent appear in the film, not by the date on which they were shot. A special section: James Dean: Behind the Camera, follows the photographs from his films. They represent photographs that Dean took himself, on the sets of these films.

Here then, is our celebration of James Dean. He lives on.

LEITH ADAMS, KEITH BURNS
Los Angeles, July 1990

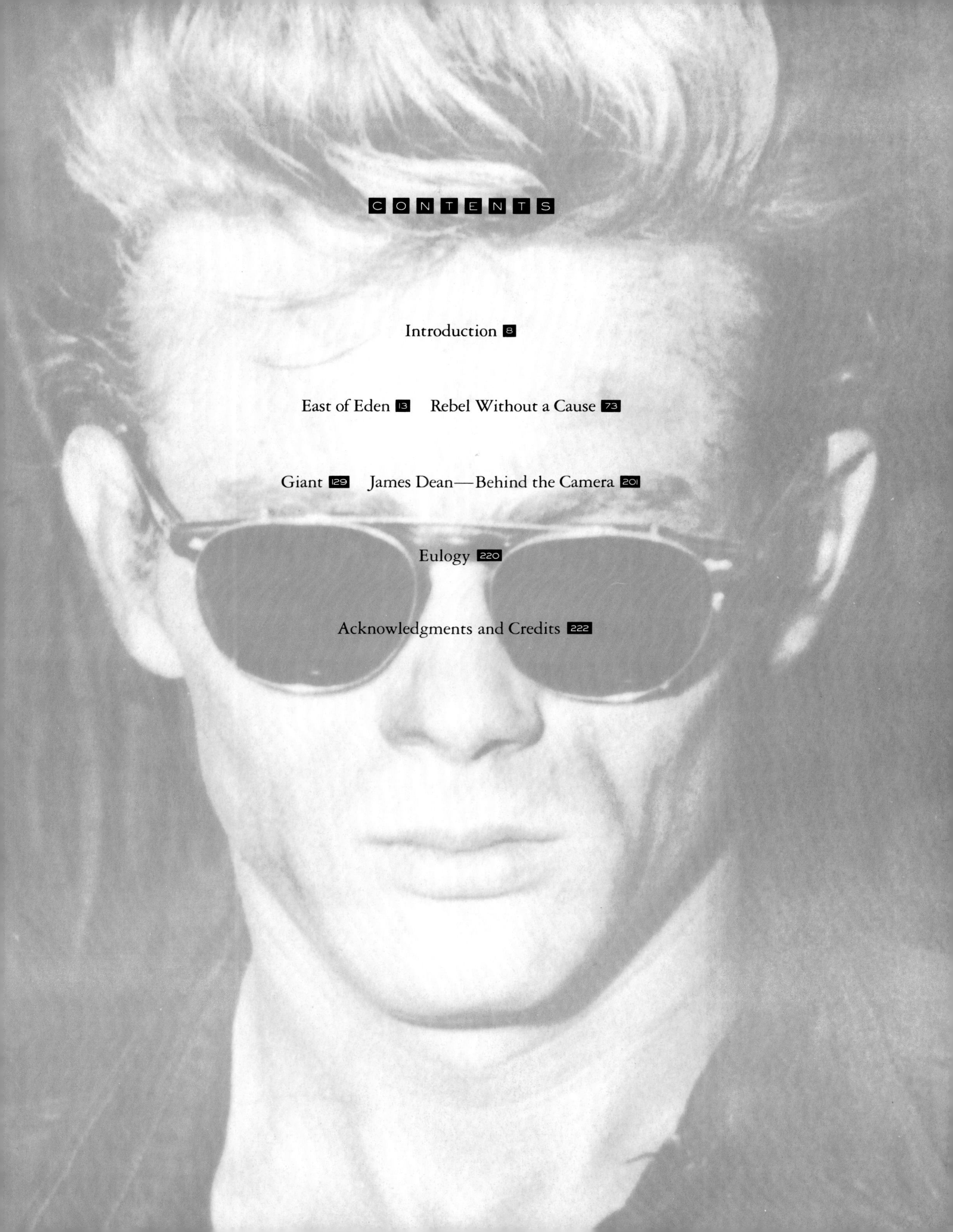

CONTENTS

INTRODUCTION

by Dennis Hopper

I'd starred in a television show called *Medic* entitled "Boy in a Storm." I played an epileptic. This show aired January 5, 1955. I was 18 years old. Seven studios called my agent wanting to put me under contract. Warner Bros. seemed the most interesting. They told me there was a good chance, since George Stevens had seen the show, of me playing the son of Rock Hudson and Elizabeth Taylor in *Giant,* but that wouldn't shoot for a year. So if Nick Ray would agree to put me in *Rebel Without a Cause,* they would give me a seven year term contract. I had the meeting at Warners with Nick. He said yes, I could be in *Rebel,* and I went under contract.

After being guaranteed that I would be in *Rebel Without a Cause,* I went to see *East of Eden* which was my first experience of seeing James Dean on screen. I thought he was interesting, but imitating Brando. My first vision of Dean was walking with my agent down a hall at Warner Bros., slouching, unshaven, black turtleneck, old Levis, sneakers, thick horn-rimmed glasses, messed hair, skulking head down, sliding by us. My agent whispered,"That's James Dean." I turned around, looked after him and exclaimed in a loud voice, "That's James Dean?"

Later the same day, we went across from Warner Bros. to the drugstore. Jimmy was sitting hunched over a cup of coffee. He was filling his spoon with sugar and, as he dipped it, watching the sugar slowly dissolve into the black coffee, and then filling the spoon and dipping it again, continuing the action over and over and over again. People were talking to him, but he was concentrating only on the spoon and sugar, never responding to their continuous dialogue. He looked not unsimilar to a junkie waiting for his connection on 42nd Street. When my agent introduced me, he didn't turn or even make an audible grunt of recognition.

One of my first jobs, since James Dean was in New York, was to play Jim Stark in the screen test with all of the girls who were tested, everyone from Jayne Mansfield to Natalie Wood. Natalie and I became very close friends, practically inseparable for the next five years. Nick Adams and I moved into a house together. Nicholas Ray and I came close to having a fist fight over Natalie at the chickie run. We were both having affairs with her.

That same night I grabbed James Dean and threw him into a car and told him that I had to know what he was doing as an actor. Because until seeing him I thought I was the greatest young actor in the world, and I didn't understand his method of working. He asked me if I hated my family. I said that yes, I was very angry with them. He said, "Yes, me too. That's our drive to act." I said that when my parents would show up at the theater I would be very angry, and would feel like saying, "I'm going to show you. I'm going to be somebody." The only thing that was real to them was my becoming a doctor, a lawyer, or an engineer. They felt that pursuing an acting career meant failure. He said he felt the same way when his mother died. He went to her grave and cried, "Mother, why did you leave me." and that turned into "Mother, I hate you. I'll

show you. I'll be somebody." So our drive has the same beginning, misguided anger and hate, and wanting to communicate through play acting and creating.

James Dean became my personal acting coach, and we went on to do *Giant* together. He told me you are technically proficient, you give line readings better than most actors, you study, and you're full of preconceived ideas. You must forget this and learn a new way of working. You must start to do things and not show them. You must not act smoking a cigarette or drinking a drink, you must simply do it. In the beginning, when you're in front of a camera or on a stage doing these simple realities it will be very difficult, you will be self conscious, but then it will become natural. You must remember you're as real as the people watching, you're real and your audience is real. You must not indicate. You must get rid of all of your preconceived ideas. You must do things, not show things. When someone knocks on the door, you must go and open it, then you see that they have a gun in their hand, and then you react. Simple reality is when you say hello to someone and they say "Go fuck yourself," and then you react. But the next time you say "hello" their response might be a hello with a smile. Your hello must not indicate how you know they are going to respond to you. Many mornings on *Giant* I would say hello to Jimmy and he wouldn't respond at all, but walk right on by, deep in concentration.

I have never seen an actor as dedicated, with the extreme concentration and exceptional imagination as James Dean. He could take the written imaginary circumstance and make it his own by improvising–lying on the ground in a fetal position playing with a wound-up toy monkey beating its cymbals, giggling while being searched in the police station because it tickled, standing up in a drunken daze making the sound of sirens with his arms outstretched, hitting his fists into the sergeant's desk, jumping off a diving board into a swimming pool with no water, or doing the voice of Mr. Magoo throughout the movie, which was the voice of Jim Backus, his father in *Rebel*–things that were not written on the page, things that were invented by the actor.

Before starting every scene Jimmy would go off into a corner, holding his head, pacing, doing what at that time was called preparing for a scene or doing his preparation. Then he would tell Nick when he was ready to begin. Later when we were doing *Giant*, I had the opportunity to ask Jimmy what he was doing. Jimmy said most of the time he was trying to clear his mind and approach the scene as if it were for the first time. The most important thing for an actor or an athlete is to be relaxed.

When working with Elizabeth Taylor, in his first scene with her in Texas there were about a thousand people roped off a hundred yards from the scene. Jimmy walked away in the middle of this first take half way toward the people, pulled out his cock and pissed, and then went back and did the scene. When we were driving back to the hotel that night I said, "Jimmy, I've seen you do a lot of crazy things, but this one I just don't understand." He said, "Well, I was so nervous because of Liz I could barely speak. So I figured if I could go and piss before a thousand people I could go back and do anything in front of the camera."

He had me watch him closely as he grew older and aged in the part of Jett Rink. I remember him being very concerned with the scene he had with Carroll Baker in the bar when he asks her to marry him. Jimmy was 25 playing a 65 year old man. He had me stand and watch and he would come to me and ask if I believed he was an old man. I told him he looked so old I'm sure an audience would feel that the Carroll Baker character was quite safe because he wouldn't be able to get it up to fuck. He seemed satisfied with that observation, and it was an honest one.

James Dean was the most intense actor and human being I've ever met. People either loved him or hated him. He could eliminate the terms like or dislike or he's o.k. I never heard them uttered in reference to Jimmy. His idols were Montgomery Clift and Marlon Brando. He said he had Clift in his lowered left hand saying, "Please forgive me," and Brando in his raised right hand saying, "Go fuck yourself," and James Dean was somewhere in the middle.

He said it didn't matter how your lines came out or

what crazy kind of behavior you did with your characters. He said you could do Hamlet's soliloquy walking on your hands and eating a carrot as long as an audience could see your eyes and believe you, that your feelings when you are an honest actor show through your eyes.

Jimmy was also very nearsighted. He could barely see four feet in front of him. He thought that it helped him tremendously as an actor because he had to imagine everything that was happening beyond that point. I remember sitting in the commissary at Warner Bros. at a table with Jimmy and Natalie, and Dick Davalos, who played Jimmy's brother in *East of Eden*, came and joined our party. I thought Jimmy was being very rude to Davalos. He didn't say hello and didn't acknowledge his presence. When Dick started having a conversation with Natalie, Jimmy said, "Davalos, is that you?" Dick said, "Yea, it's me," sarcastically. Jimmy said, "Wow man, it's you," and he got up and hugged him. "I couldn't see you man, I left my glasses in the trailer." I'm not sure whether Davalos, who had been sitting at the table for ten minutes, ever believed him or thought he was just doing a number.

I remember walking outside the commissary at Warners with Jimmy and Jack Warner came up with a major world banker named Mr. Semenenko. Jack Warner had talked his brother Harry into selling Warner Bros. to Semenenko. Semenenko had owned the studio for one week, then Jack had bought it back, screwing his brother out of half ownership of Warner Bros. Mr. Warner enthusiastically introduced Mr. Semenenko to Jimmy. Mr. Semenenko reached out his hand to shake hands, and Jimmy reached into his pocket and pulled out a handful of change, threw it at their feet and turned and walked away. I was shocked, not knowing the story, and I just looked at the two men, then turned and followed Jimmy.

I find it unfortunate that the two biographies that have been written about James Dean say that he was gay. James Dean was not gay. The two great loves of his life in Hollywood were Pier Angeli and Ursula Andress. Pier Angeli married Vic Damone. Jimmy sat in the rain on his motorcycle outside the church. She'd asked Jimmy to marry her. He'd asked her to wait until he saw how his career was going. Ursula Andress met John Derek and proceeded to parade him on the set of *Giant* after Jimmy refused to marry her for the same reason.

Jimmy was not only an internal actor but an expressionist, which came partly from his studying dance. He would physicalize actions, such as the way he lifted himself up on the windmill in *Giant*, or goose-stepped measuring off the land, or his sleight of hand gesture as Jett Rink. He had the amazing capacity to pick up and learn a new trick almost immediately, tossing a rope and making a knot, a card trick from a magician, coin tricks, racing a car.

In my opinion James Dean directed *Rebel Without a Cause*, from blocking all the scenes, setting the camera, starting the scene, and saying "cut." Nicholas Ray intelligently allowed him to do this.

George Stevens and Jimmy fought from the first day on. Jimmy insisted upon doing long, drawn out behavioral sequences that Stevens knew he would not be able to use in the film. Stevens finally told Jimmy that he should take his little 8mm camera and go out and shoot his own movies, because he was going to make sure that he, Jimmy, was never going to work in Hollywood again. Jimmy was called in before dawn to apply his makeup as an old man in *Giant*. Stevens kept him in his trailer all day and he didn't work. Jimmy told him that night if that ever happened again he would not show up for a day. The next day it happened again. It was on a Friday. Jimmy didn't show up for work on Saturday. Stevens was ready to use him at 7 am. The studio went crazy. They couldn't find him all day Saturday, or Sunday, our day off. Monday morning Jimmy was back in makeup. Jack Warner and Steve Trilling (head of production) and George Stevens called Jimmy into Warner's office. They screamed and yelled about the responsibilities of the actor and how much it cost production every day whether the cameras rolled or not. The tirade continued for about 20 minutes. The three men fell silent. Jimmy took his feet off the table where he had propped them up and said, "Are you finished, because I want to tell you something. I'm

not a fucking machine that you can turn on and off. I come in there every day prepared to do the scenes for that day. Sometimes I've stayed up all night to be tired enough to play this old alcoholic. This time it was one day, the next time it's going to be two days, and then you can start counting the weeks." Not waiting for an answer, he stood up and exited.

A week before Jimmy died he went into a silent order Catholic monastery for three days. Stevens made him promise that he would not race the Porsche Spyder that he had spent his entire *Giant* salary to purchase. I believe it was around $17,000. We weren't finished shooting, but Jimmy had finished principal photography. Later Nick Adams would be asked to dub Dean's voice in the drunk scene in the banquet room of the hotel because Stevens felt his performance was inaudible.

Jimmy came back from the monastery clean shaven, with a haircut, wearing a suit and tie. In the year that I had known Jimmy I'd never seen him personally wear a suit and tie. He came to me and said goodbye. I found this rather curious and later found out that he had said goodbye to a number of people. I would have gone to the race with him, but I had to stay and work. I still found the way he said goodbye bizarre and strange.

My agent asked me to go to the theater. I was sitting in the audience, waiting for the play to begin. Someone came and got my agent and he went to the lobby. When he came back he said, "I have something to tell you but you must promise me that you won't leave the theater." By his behavior and the look on his face I was certain that someone in my family was dead. When he told me that James Dean had died in a car accident, I hit him, muttered the word liar. The lights in the theater went off and a single spotlight came up on an empty stage. It seemed like an eternity before I ran from the theater. I thought he must have grandstanded out on one of the turns in the race. I'd seen him go between cars, hit haybales and bounce out in front a few times when he won in Palm Springs, right after *Rebel.* I was confused when I heard later that he died in a simpleminded stupid crash on the highway because someone didn't stop at a stop sign.

The notions of James Dean being suicidal are stupid and false. He was given a ticket for going 120 mph in a car that would go 180 mph, one hour before the crash, but he was only doing 70 mph when a man named Turnipseed ran a stop sign and Jimmy hit him. He lived. Rolf, James Dean's German mechanic, who had been sitting next to Jimmy wearing a seatbelt lived to become the head mechanic at Mercedes Benz in Germany. Jimmy died. He didn't believe in wearing a seatbelt. He thought it would be better to be thrown free of the machinery.

His death began a series of seances with all of his friends that I've never before or since experienced in my lifetime. Whether in the hysteria of the moment or the youthful pain of the experience, all of us were convinced that we'd had encounters with him.

Elizabeth Taylor came to work on the set everyday. She would start crying hysterically and would have to be sedated. It was three weeks before she was able to complete the last scene for *Giant.*

I'd like to clear up one controversy. Most people remember seeing *Rebel Without a Cause* before Dean died, but Jimmy was only a star to those of us in the industry who knew him in New York and Los Angeles. *East of Eden* was not a commercial success. *Rebel Without a Cause* had not been released yet. Natalie, Nick and I went out and promoted it throughout the country. After its tremendous success, *East of Eden* was re-released to become a commercial success and then *Giant.*

Every time I go to Europe I remember that James Dean never saw Europe, but yet I see his face everywhere. There's James Dean, Humphrey Bogart, and Marilyn Monroe—windows of the Champs Élyseés, discos in the south of Spain, restaurants in Sweden, t-shirts in Moscow.

My life was confused and disoriented for years by his passing. My sense of destiny destroyed—the great films he would have directed, the great performances he would have given, the great humanitarian he would have become, and yet, he's the greatest actor and star I have ever known.

son. I didn't like the expression on his face, so I kept him waiting. I also wanted to see how he'd react to that. It seemed that I'd outtoughed him, because when I called him into my office, he'd dropped the belligerent pose. We tried to talk, but conversation was not his gift, so we sat looking at each other. He asked me if I wanted to ride on the back of his motorbike. I didn't enjoy the ride. He was showing off–a country boy not impressed with big-city traffic. When I got back to the office, I called Paul and told him this kid actually was Cal in *East of Eden*; no sense looking further or "reading" him. I sent Dean to see Steinbeck...John thought Dean a snotty kid. I said that was irrelevant; wasn't he Cal? John said he sure as hell was, and that was it." ELIA KAZAN

(Elia Kazan: A Life Alfred A. Knopf New York 1988)

EAST OF EDEN

"Elia Kazan's struggles to raise adult themes in the movies always created conflicts with Hollywood's censors in the Breen Office. Beginning with PINKY in 1949, A STREETCAR NAMED DESIRE in 1950 and now EAST OF EDEN in 1954, Kazan focused on issues that the censors wished Hollywood would overlook."

Motion Picture Association of America, Inc.
8480 Beverly Boulevard
Hollywood 48, California
WEbster 3-7101

MPAA

Eric Johnston
President

Joseph I. Breen
Vice President and Director
Production Code Administration

December 2, 1953

Mr. J.L. Warner
Warner Bros. Pictures, Inc.
4000 W. Olive Avenue
Burbank, California

Dear Mr. Warner:

This goes to you in confirmation of our conference yesterday with Messrs. Steve Trilling, Finlay McDermid and Walter MacEwen with regard to the first draft script of the Steinbeck novel, EAST OF EDEN. The purpose of the conference was to discuss the fact that the present script contains material which could not be approved under the requirements of the Production Code.

This unacceptable material has to do with the various scenes laid in a brothel. As we explained in some detail, it has been the steadfast procedure of the Code Administration not to approve scenes dealing with any of the mechanics of prostitution. This would include scenes laid in or around brothels.

This procedure of ours was given official sanction by the Board of Directors of the Association in the case of our rejection of the Italian picture THE BICYCLE THIEF, which contained a scene laid in a brothel. Our contention that this type of material was not suitable for the mixed family audiences to which our pictures appeal was unanimously sustained by the Board.

When we discussed this story previously with Mr. Trilling and Mr. McDermid and Mr. Kazan about a year ago, we agreed that it would be acceptable to establish the fact that Adam's wife had become a prostitute. But we endeavored to make it clear at that time that we did not feel that we could go any further than merely establishing the fact, which is necessary to bring about

Warner - Page 2 December 2, 1953

the climactic tragedy of the story. At the conference yesterday, we discussed certain tentative ideas as to how this objective could be attained and still steer clear of any unacceptable exploitation of brothels or prostitution.

Whenever you feel it advisable to discuss this matter any further, we should be happy to place ourselves at your convenience.

There is one other element in the script which is also unacceptable. This arises from the attitude of the Sheriff and possibly others in the town, who seem to condone the existence of the brothel, merely because it is well managed and orderly. Naturally, under the requirements of the Code, we could not approve any dialogue which seemed to condone or justify organized prostitution.

Cordially yours,

Joseph I. Breen

cc Trilling

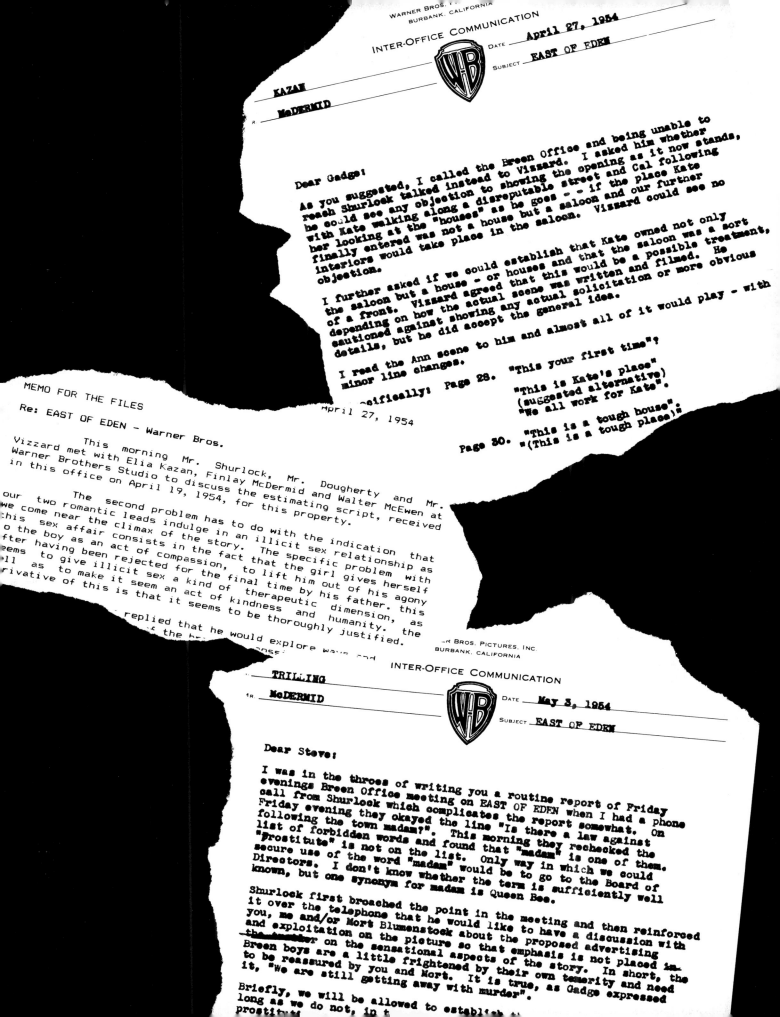

WARNER BROS. ...
BURBANK, CALIFORNIA

INTER-OFFICE COMMUNICATION

... KAZAN
...R. McDERMID

DATE April 27, 1954
SUBJECT EAST OF EDEN

Dear Gadge:

As you suggested, I called the Breen Office and being unable to reach Shurlock talked instead to Vizzard. I asked him whether he could see any objection to showing the opening as it now stands, with Kate walking along a disreputable street and Cal following her looking at the "houses" as he goes - - if the place Kate finally entered was not a house but a saloon and our further interiors would take place in the saloon. Vizzard could see no objection.

I further asked if we could establish that Kate owned not only the saloon but a house - or houses and that the saloon was a sort of a front. Vizzard agreed that this would be a possible treatment, depending on how the actual scene was written and filmed. He cautioned against showing any actual solicitation or more obvious details, but he did accept the general idea.

I read the Ann scene to him and almost all of it would play - with minor line changes.

...ecifically: Page 28. "This your first time"?
"This is Kate's place"
(suggested alternative)
"We all work for Kate".

Page 30. "This is a tough house".
"(This is a tough place)"

MEMO FOR THE FILES

April 27, 1954

Re: EAST OF EDEN - Warner Bros.

This morning Mr. Shurlock, Mr. Dougherty and Mr. Vizzard met with Elia Kazan, Finlay McDermid and Walter McEwen at Warner Brothers Studio to discuss the estimating script, received in this office on April 19, 1954, for this property.

The second problem has to do with the indication that ...our two romantic leads indulge in an illicit sex relationship as we come near the climax of the story. The specific problem with ...this sex affair consists in the fact that the girl gives herself ...o the boy as an act of compassion, to lift him out of his agony ...fter having been rejected for the final time by his father. this ...eems to give illicit sex a kind of therapeutic dimension, as ...ll as to make it seem an act of kindness and humanity. the ...rivative of this is that it seems to be thoroughly justified.

... replied that he would explore ways and ...f the ...

...R BROS. PICTURES, INC.
BURBANK, CALIFORNIA

INTER-OFFICE COMMUNICATION

... TRILLING
...R. McDERMID

DATE May 3, 1954
SUBJECT EAST OF EDEN

Dear Steve:

I was in the throes of writing you a routine report of Friday evenings Breen Office meeting on EAST OF EDEN when I had a phone call from Shurlock which complicates the report somewhat. On Friday evening they okayed the line "Is there a law against following the town madam?". This morning they rechecked the list of forbidden words and found that "madam" is one of them. "Prostitute" is not on the list. Only way in which we could secure use of the word "madam" would be to go to the Board of Directors. I don't know whether the term is sufficiently well known, but one synonym for madam is Queen Bee.

Shurlock first broached the point in the meeting and then reinforced it over the telephone that he would like to have a discussion with you, me and/or Mort Blumenstock about the proposed advertising and exploitation on the picture so that emphasis is not placed ~~in the...~~ on the sensational aspects of the story. In short, the Breen boys are a little frightened by their own temerity and need to be reassured by you and Mort. It is true, as Gadge expressed it, "We are still getting away with murder".

Briefly, we will be allowed to establish ... long as we do not, in t... prostitu...

ELIA KAZAN

Dear Jack: Just a note to say goodbye and to thank you for Your understanding. The WATERFRONT movie did take a lot longer than I figured - or than you likely figured. But you never sowacked (how the hell do you spell that word??) about the delay. I appreciate. I leave by boat tomorrow and will be ready to go to work in real earnest in four weeks. I'll come right out there and stay.

About casting. I think Dean is o.k. Impress on him or have some one impress on him again when he arrives out there, the great importance of living an outdoor life, sunshine exercise food and fucking. Just all the healthy things, and lots of sleep. He's an odd kid and I think we should make him as handsome as possible.

I consider the kid: Dick Davlos a fair possibility for Aron. I'm not nuts about him, but there is something nice about him and perhaps he can do it. I think Solly should immediately start looking out there to match Dean. There was a kid in California I once used as a child Thespian: Darryl Kickman. But I think a more possible field would be the little theatres, college theatres etc. Now that we have Dean we can match him. Dick Davlos isn't going to run away, and if we cant do better we can always use him.

About Abra. Julie Harris is a brilliant actress. She is very possibly too old. A friend of mine Gjon Mili (the famous Life Photographer) is doing a test of her and Dean, photographic only, this coming week. He is a sensitive person and if he cant make Dean and Julie Harris match no one can. But I dont in any case want Abra to look older than Cal. Of the three girls I tested in New York I like Joanne Woodward best. She is in the possible but not enthusiastic quality.

Kate could be KAY MEDFORD. a brilliant new actress in New York. I advised Harry Mayer to "put a string on her". But you might have some one remind him again.

For the old man I'm still interested in getting an old western star. But, what about Gary Cooper? He has been quoted as saying that he'd do anything I wanted to do with him. Most of that kind of talk is strictly for the cocktail hour. But Cooper seems like a very sincere guy. I'd like to have him very much and could even build the part up a little - a little, only a little - for him. Then there is Freddie March. I'd rather have an outdoor type.

I'd still like Harry Stradling, but they tell me he's gone to Rome for a long time. Could Steve check on this. Second choice: Russ Metty. Jim Wong Howe. I don't want Sam Leavitt

I still dont know whether I'm going to do it part on location or what? First thing I do after I check in and check a few things is to take the night train to Salinas and look around up there a couple of days. John Steinbeck told me where there were some old streets.

I think the whole script needs about forty pages taken out of it, and moved outdoors more etc. But that can all wait.

mail me your reactions to N.Y. City

free!

March 10th, 1954

Dear Gadg:

Thanks for your letter. I sympathize with your trials and tribulations on WATERFRONT. However, now that it is behind you, with the rest you are going to get you will come out "fit as a fiddle and ready for love".

About the boy, Dean, inasmuch as your impression of him is a good one, we naturally will go along with you. You said he is an odd kid. I hope he isn't too odd as it is getting to the point now that when we make pictures with odd people, the whole machine is thrown out of order. You know it only takes one odd spark plug to make the motor miss. I, too, am fed up with people who are too odd. That doesn't mean Marlon Brando is odd. I am sure he knows the score and just makes everything tough in order to make himself different. However, the hell with Brando. He was in a picture called, THE WILD ONE and even the operators refused to stay in the booth. As our good pal, Billy Shakespeare said virtually 500 years ago, "The Play is Still the Thing".

Solly Baiano and Bill Orr are going to work on the casting problem. Julie Harris is a great talent and we are anxiously awaiting the Gjon Mili test. Re: the cameraman, we will end up with someone you like and who has ability. I like your idea of going to Salinas as soon as you get here. However, I like your idea best that the script needs to be boiled down and forty pages taken out. Right now, I will settle for thirty-five. Every good wish from Steve and the gang.

Sincerely,

Mr. E. Kazan
167 E. 74th St.
New York, New York

CLASS OF SERVICE
This is a full-rate Telegram or Cablegram unless its deferred character is indicated by a suitable symbol above or preceding the address.

WESTERN UNION

W. P. MARSHALL, PRESIDENT

FX-1201

SYMBOLS
DL=Day Letter
NL=Night Letter
LT=Int'l Letter Telegram
VLT=Int'l Victory Ltr.

The filing time shown in the date line on telegrams and day letters is STANDARD TIME at point of origin. Time of receipt is STANDARD TIME at point of destination

WG-14. 1 NEW YORK NY FEB. 5, 1954.

KAZAN (VIA MAYER) TO JL ------ FOUND NEW BOY THAT I MOST ENTHUS-ASTIC ABOUT AND WHO, COULD MAKE PICTURE THIS SPRING SO WE DONT HAVE TO WAIT. UNTIL JUNE. ALSO HAVE GIRL I LIKE AND WILL TEST BOTH OF THEM WEEK FROM TUESDAY.

THE COMPANY WILL APPRECIATE SUGGESTIONS FROM ITS PATRONS CON...

CLASS OF SERVICE
This is a full-rate Telegram or Cablegram unless its deferred character is indicated by a suitable symbol above or preceding the address.

WESTERN UNION

W. P. MARSHALL, PRESIDENT

FX-1201

SYMBOLS
DL=Day Letter
NL=Night Letter
LT=Int'l Letter Telegram
VLT=Int'l Victory Ltr.

The filing time shown in the date line on telegrams and day letters is STANDARD TIME at point of origin. Time of receipt is STANDARD TIME at point of destination

WG-1. 1 NEW YORK NY FEB. 8, 1954.

MAYER TO TRILLING AND ORR ------ KAZAN DESIRES SEE TEST FILM JIMMY DEAN LEE PHILLIPS. ALSO TEST LUCY ANN MCALEER WITH KARL MALDEN. PLEASE AIR EXPRESS SOON AS POSSIBLE.

...TIONS FROM ITS PATRO...

CLASS OF SERVICE
This is a full-rate Telegram or Cablegram unless its deferred character is indicated by a suitable symbol above or preceding the address.

WESTERN UNION

W. P. MARSHALL, PRESIDENT

FX-1201

SYMBOLS
DL=Day Letter
NL=Night Letter
LT=Int'l Letter Telegram
VLT=Int'l Victory Ltr.

The filing time shown in the date line on telegrams and day letters is STANDARD TIME at point of origin. Time of receipt is STANDARD TIME at point of destination

WG-2. NEW YORK NY FEB. 11, 1954.

KAZAN (VIA MAYER) TO JL (CONFIDENTIAL) ------ DEAR JACK: DID NOT HAVE GOOD REACTION WILLIAMS SCRIPT BUT WILL STUDY AGAIN THIS WEEKEND AND CALL YOU FIRST OF WEEK. THINK I FOUND RIGHT BOY FOR EDEN AND TESTING TUESDAY. THRU CUTTING WATERFRONT END NEXT WEEK BUT FIRST WANT TAKE VACATION AND AFTER THAT WILL GO WORK AGAIN. THOROUGHLY TIRED RIGHT NOW. BEST.

...TIONS FROM ITS PATRONS CONCERNING ITS SERVICE

"THE DISCOVERY OF JAMES DEAN BY ELIA KAZAN AND WARNER BROS. IS REFLECTED IN THESE TELEGRAMS FROM STEVE TRILLING'S FILES: THE JACK L. WARNER COLLECTION, USC CINEMA-TELEVISION LIBRARY. TRILLING, EXECUTIVE ASSISTANT TO JACK WARNER, FOR HIS OWN PERSONAL REFERENCE, WOULD "LINE OUT" AND INITIAL EACH PIECE OF CORRESPONDENCE THAT CROSSED HIS DESK, INDICATING HE'D HANDLED THE MATTER."

FEB. 16, 1954.

MAYER TO ORR AND TRILLING ---- AIR EXPRESSING ALL BATTLE CRY TESTS
TODAY. KNOW WALLIS INTERESTED NEWMAN. IF POSSIBLE DO NOT SHOW TEST TO HIM
UNTIL COMPLETION KAZAN TEST NEWMAN EAST EDEN NEXT WEEK.

Orr

THE COMPANY WILL APPRECIATE SUGGESTIONS FROM ITS PATRONS CONCERNING ITS SERVICE

CLASS OF SERVICE

This is a full-rate Telegram or Cablegram unless its deferred character is indicated by a suitable symbol above or preceding the address.

SYMBOLS

DL=Day Letter
NL=Night Letter
LT=Int'l Letter Telegram
VLT=Int'l Victory Ltr.

FX-1201

The filing time shown in the date line on telegrams and day letters is STANDA[RD TIME at point of origin. Ti]me of receipt is STANDARD TIME at point of destination

WG-4. NEW YORK NY FEB. 23, 1954.

KAZAN (VIA MAYER) TO JL ------ SCREENED JAMES DEAN TEST YESTERDAY
AND AM SURE HE'S THE BOY FOR CAL. ALSO THOUGHT GIRL EXCELLENT AND
TESTING ANOTHER EXCELLENT GIRL TODAY. BELIEVE IF SPEND ANOTHER WEEK
HERE CAN HAVE ENTIRE MOVIE CAST BEFORE GOING ON VACATION SO DEPART-
MENTS CAN WORK ETC WHILE I AM LUXURIATING IN THE SUN. WILL SEND YOU
DEAN TEST TONIGHT AND WILL EAGERLY AWAIT YOUR REACTION. ALSO WILL
SEND BY END OF WEEK CAST AS I THINK IT SHOULD BE. FOR FATHER AND
MOTHER WOULD LOVE TO HAVE JIMMY STEWART AND BETTY FIELD. SURE BETTY
AVAILABLE. PLEASE CHECK RE STEWART. LOVE. GADGE.

THE COMPANY WILL APPRECIATE SUGGESTIONS FROM ITS PATRONS CONCERNING ITS SERVICE

CLASS OF SERVICE

This is a full-rate Telegram or Cablegram unless its deferred character is indicated by a suitable symbol above or preceding the address.

WES[TERN] UN[ION]

W. P. MA[RSHALL]

The filing time shown in the date line on telegrams and day letters is STANDAR[D]

WG-13. NEW YORK NY MAR. 1, 195[4]

MAYER TO JL ------ KAZAN ADVISES DEFINITELY USING JIMMY DEAN FOR
ROLE CAL. PROCEEDING FINALIZE CONTRACT.

THE COMPANY WILL APPRECIATE SUGGESTIONS FROM ITS PATRONS CONCERNING ITS SERVICE

SYMBOLS

DL=Day Letter
NL=Night Letter
LT=Int'l Letter Telegram
VLT=Int'l Victory Ltr.

FX-1201

Time of receipt is STANDARD TIME at point of destination

MAYER TO TRILLING ------ KAZAN AGREEABLE WE PROCEED JULIE HARRIS.
WILL KEEP YOU INFORMED. RETURNING HARRIS TEST FOR KAZAN USE. HE PLEASED
BASIVA SET. KAZAN DEAN ARRIVING AMERICAN AIRLINES FLIGHT ONE AT 555 PM
YOUR TIME APRIL 8TH. THANKS INFORMATION PAUL NEWMAN. LOCAL MCA OFFICE
AWAITING CONFIRMATION FROM WASSERMAN. MEANWHILE WE MAKING PLANS SEND HIM
COAST AFTER TV BROADCAST SUNDAY NIGHT. WILL ADVISE FLIGHT DETAILS. WILL
AWAIT WORD RE CONTRACT.

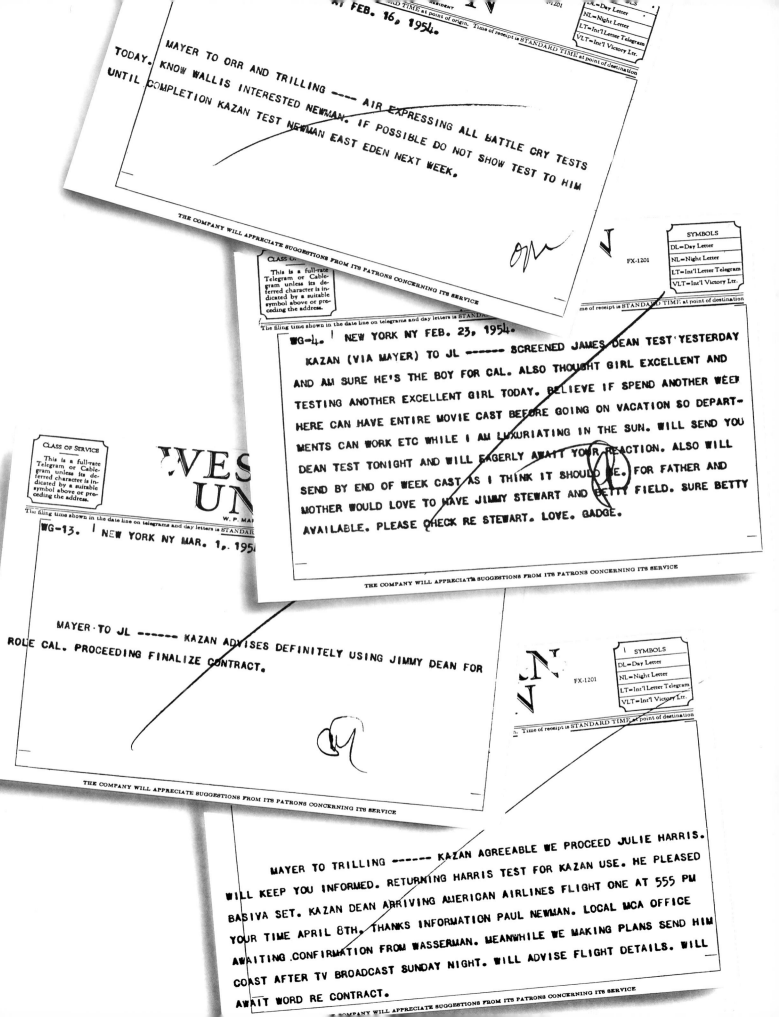

THE COMPANY WILL APPRECIATE SUGGESTIONS FROM ITS PATRONS CONCERNING ITS SERVICE

	WARNER BROS.	50%
	Pictures Present	5%
Must be 50% size of title in adv.	John Steinbeck's	50%
	"EAST OF EDEN"	100%
Must be 50% size of title in adv.	An Elia Kazan Production	50%
	Starring	
Must star on scr. & in adv. preceding Dean.	JULIE HARRIS	50%
No adv. obligation	JAMES DEAN	50%
Star on scr. & in adv.	RAYMOND MASSEY	50%
	with	
Must be in adv.	BURL IVES	25%
No adv. obligation.	RICHARD DAVALOS	25%
	JO VAN FLEET	25%
	ALBERT DEKKER	25%
	LOIS SMITH	25%
	HAROLD GORDON	10%
	LONNY CHAPMAN	10%
	in CinemaScope	50%
	in WarnerColor	50%
	Print by TECHNICOLOR	15%
No adv. obligation. use where and when space permits.	Music by Leonard Rosenman	3%
NOTE: Where possible, increase to 30%.	Screen Play by Paul Osborn	30%
	Directed by Elia Kazan	40%
FOURTH REVISED	A Warner Bros. Picture	5%

* * *

(AS O.K.'D BY J.L. WARNER

REVISED
5/25/54

"EAST OF EDEN"

Elia Kazan #810

STAFF & CAST

STAFF

Producer-Director	Elia Kazan	Ext. 771
Unit Manager	Don Page - 4355 Clybourn	Su 2-3150
Asst. Director	Horace Hough - 11633 La Maida St.	Po 6-3546
2nd Asst. "	Carter Gibson - 10955 Bluffside	Su 2-9041
3rd " "	Claude Archer - 4541 Talofa - N.H	Su 2-1354
Art Director	James Basevi - 456 Skyewiay	Ariz 7-5087
" "	Mal Bert - 436 E. Fairview Blvd.- Inglewood	Or 8-1446
Cutter	Owen Marks - 5013 Ventura Blvd.	St 4-3440
Cameraman	Ted McCord - 965 Verdugo Circle	Ci 3-6269
Operator	Andy Anderson - 4120 Brunswick	No 3-0372
Camera Asst.	Fred Terso - 5808 Willowcrest Ave.	Su 1-7972
Co-ordo.	John Hambleton - 8105 N. Wilcox - Holly.	Ho 4-5151
Camera Asst.	Wm. J. Ranaldi - 5523 Fulton - Van Nuys	St 5-5110
Script Sup.	Irva Mae Ross - 131 So. Avon -Burbank	Th 2-8955
	Idyllwild	8-0722
Dial. Dir.	Guy Thomajan	
Stillman	Jack Albin - 846 N. Fairfax	Ho 4-0255
Gaffer	Charles O'Bannon - 2701 Laurel Canyon	Ho 3-8324
Best Boy	Ernest Long - 1115 N. Avon St.	Th 6-1638
Grip	William Classen-3553 Rosemary St.(Glendale)	Ch 9-1038
Set Dresser	Bill Wallace - 3100 Clark St.	Th 6-2959
Prop Man	Red Turner - 3734 S. Norton Ave.	Ax 4-8479
Asst. Prop Man	George Sweeney - 4039 LaSalle St.	Ve 8-4685
Mixer	Stanley Jones - 4536 Arcola Ave.	Su 1-3754
Recorder	Ed McDonald - 3322 Charleston Way	Ho 4-5217
Boom Boy	Everet Hughes - 17190 Lassen St.	Di 3-4085
Wardrobe Man	Leon Roberts - 7570½ DeLongpre	Ho 5-0011
" Woman	Ora Johnson - 6314 Morella	Su 3-5792
Hairdresser	Tillie Starriet - 5446 Woodman	St 5-4494
Makeup Man	Robert Ewing - 11912 Riverside Dr.	Su 2-8763
Secretary-to Mr. Kazan	Rhea Burakoff - 8241 DeLongpre	Ho 5-2585
		Ext. 771

CAST

"Adam"	Raymond Massey	
"Abra"	Julie Harris - 3300 Riverside Dr.	Th 8-3075
"Cal Trask"	James Dean - 3908 W. Olive - Apt. 3	Th 2-5752
		Ariz 8-2018
"Aaron Trask"	Dick Davalos - " " " " "	Th 2-5752
"Kate"	Jo VanFleet - 3300 Riverside Dr.	Th 2-5892
"Will	Albert Dekker - 240 Bently Circle	Ariz 9-6758
"Ann"	Lois Smith-3401 W. Olive (Studio Motel)-	Th 6-6940
"Rantani"	Nick Dennis- 1030½ Cory Ave.	Cr 4-3962
"Joe"	Timothy Carey - 148 E. 75th St.	Cr 5-7203
	(Carlos Dvarado)	
"Sam"	Berle Ives - Bev. Wilshire Hotel	
"Mr. Albrecht"	Harold Gordon	
"Roy"	Lonnie Chapman	
"Piscora"		

E. G. STACEY

James Dean and Julie Harris pose for pre-production wardrobe tests for the first scenes of East of Eden. Note that the dark sweater and shoes Dean wears in this test were changed for lighter colored articles in the actual film.

A less than enthusiastic James Dean (Cal Trask) and a hidden Richard Davalos (as his brother Aron) pose with Jo Van Fleet's costume. The camera assistant blocking Davalos holds a color chart which is used as a reference when printing the film.

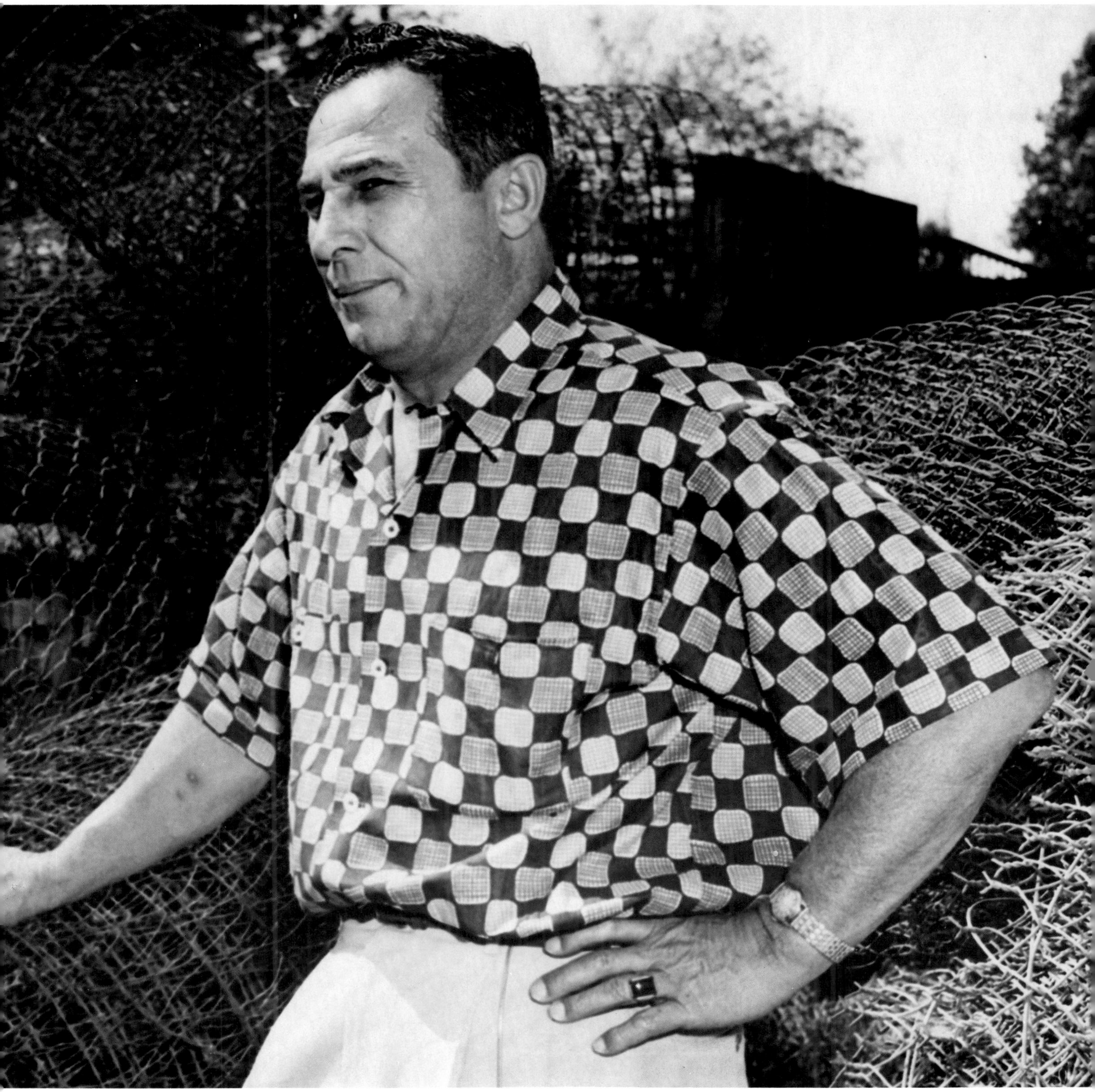

ON THE BACKLOT OF WARNER BROS. STUDIO, IN BURBANK, CALIFORNIA, THE PUBLICITY DEPARTMENT POSED JAMES DEAN FOR A SERIES OF NOW LEGENDARY PHOTOGRAPHS TO ANNOUNCE THEIR NEW STAR. A SHOT OF DEAN'S HEAD, SURROUNDED BY A SWIRL OF FENCEWIRE, IS ONE OF THE MOST FAMOUS. THIS IS HOW IT WAS DONE.

James Dean observes life from the ground up. In the first photograph, director Elia Kazan is obviously amused at Dean's unique viewpoint. The unsuspecting passersby in the next two photos have no idea of the legend-to-be lying at their feet.

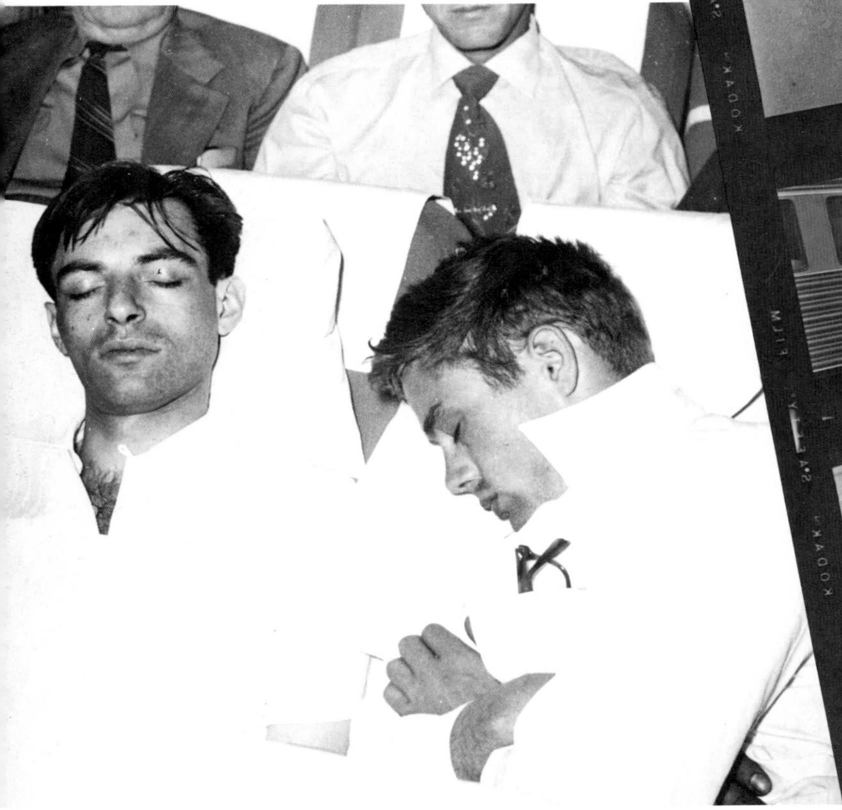

On Wednesday, May 26, 1954, cast and crew flew to Mendocino in northern California where the "Monterey" scenes were filmed. Composer Leonard Rosenman and James Dean catch some sleep on the flight north.

"I really loved him. And I really loved working with him. It was a unique experience in my life. I never worked with an actor again that was quite that way."

Julie Harris

Cinematographer Ted McCord checks the quality of light for James Dean in Mendocino.

James Dean and Timothy Carey (Joe) work out their confrontation scene in front of Kate's "house"...

JOE Now look, why're you followin' Kate around? What's the idea, squirt?

Between takes, James Dean looks…

leaps…

launches…

LOUNGES.

JAMES DEAN IN THE ICE HOUSE.

"Dean couldn't budge the huge block of ice until Elia Kazan made a derogatory remark about Dean's acting ability. The trick worked. Dean was so incensed that in a fit of anger he picked up the ice and threw it to the ground below."

Warner Bros. Publicity Release

Ted Ashton: 6/23/54

Looking down on the "Bible-reading" scene as Elia Kazan (top) rehearses Raymond Massey (left) and James Dean (right) in their parts as righteous father and rebellious son.

On a chilly night in Mendocino, Elia Kazan and James Dean sip hot drinks and try to stay warm on the front porch of Kate's "house."

Burl Ives—as the understanding Sheriff of Monterey—consoles James Dean's troubled Cal, giving him advice about the mother who left him so long ago.

James Dean and Lydia Guerero await direction from Elia Kazan beside the railroad tracks outside Salinas, California.

James Dean, back in action following his discussion with Kazan, finds another able conversationalist in actor-friend Nick Dennis who plays Rantani the bean farmer.

"Kazan insisted that Dean climb a rope, race around the gym and then run downstairs into the scene in the locker room. Unfortunately, the youthful Dean was in such good physical condition that he had to negotiate six round trips before he was sufficiently breathless to meet Kazan's requirements." Warner Bros. Publicity Release Ted Ashton: 6/4/54.

The camera crew lines up for the tracking shot of Cal and Kate talking and walking as Elia Kazan leaves the set.

James Dean throws a friendly arm around propman George Sweeney on the Warner Bros. Mid-western Street during a break in the "parade" sequence.

Waiting for the parade to begin...James Dean and kids.

"Then Jimmy bought a motorbike...I told him I didn't want to chance an accident, and that he absolutely couldn't ride the bike until the film was over."

Elia Kazan

Elia Kazan lines up a shot of James Dean watching his crop grow as cinematographer Ted McCord looks on.

JAMES DEAN... RINGS THE BELL.

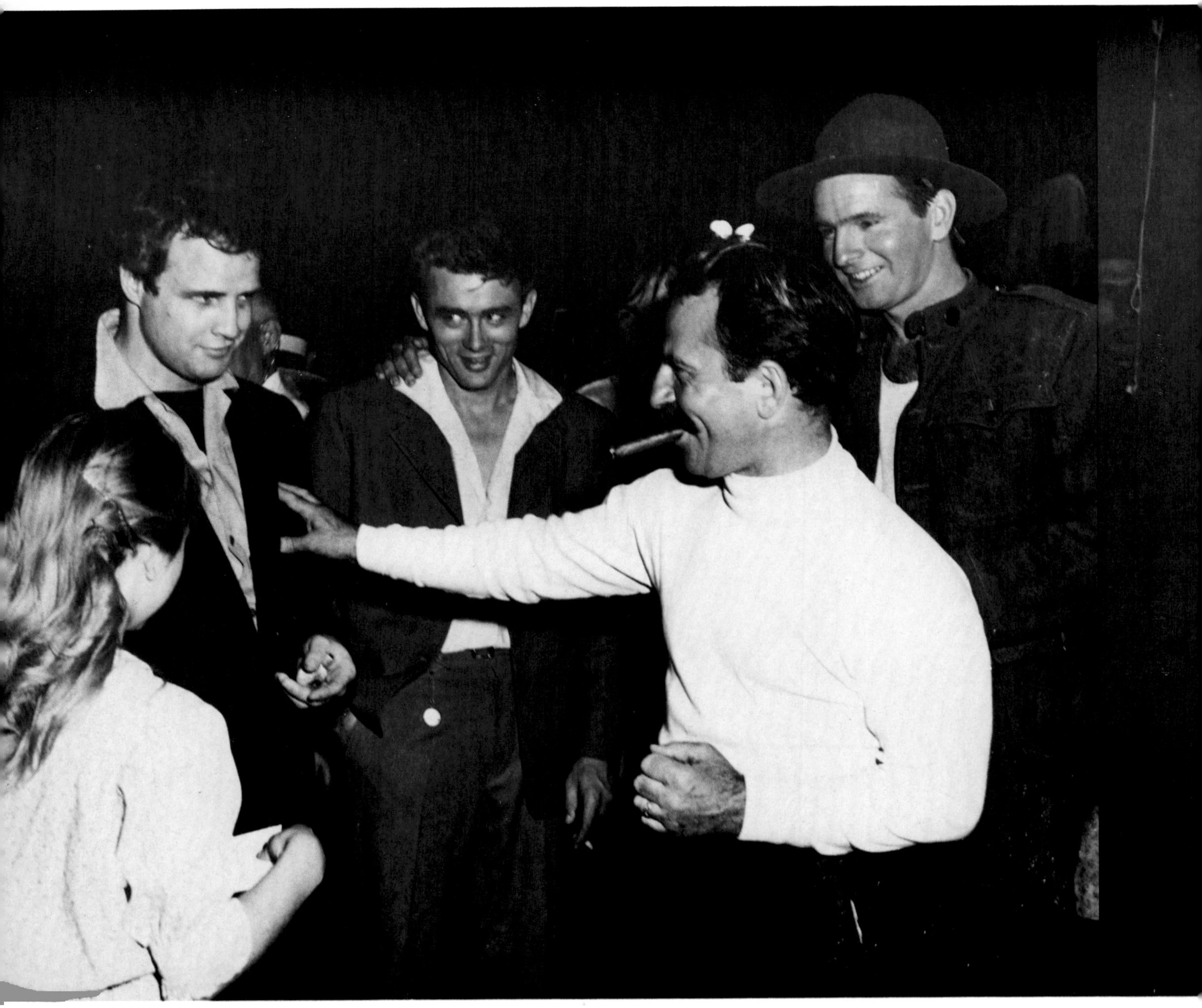

NICK DENNIS PICKS A FIGHT...

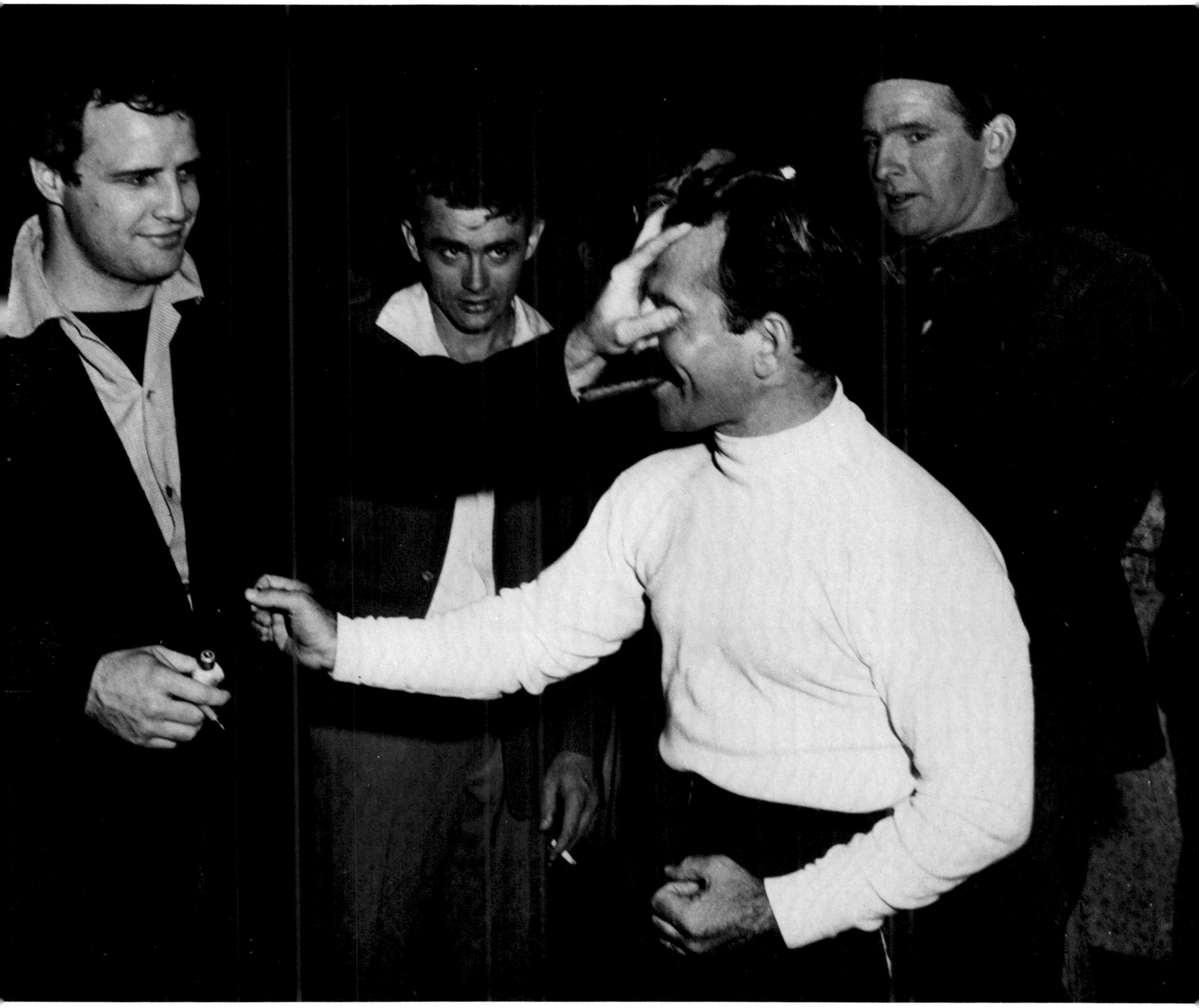

...WITH THE WRONG ACTOR. NOTE THE CHANGES IN EXPRESSION OF JAMES DEAN AND THE "SOLDIER" AS AN IMMOBILE MARLON BRANDO GRABS NICK DENNIS BY THE FACE.

As James Dean looks on, Elia Kazan instructs an elderly extra for her motion picture debut on the carnival set.

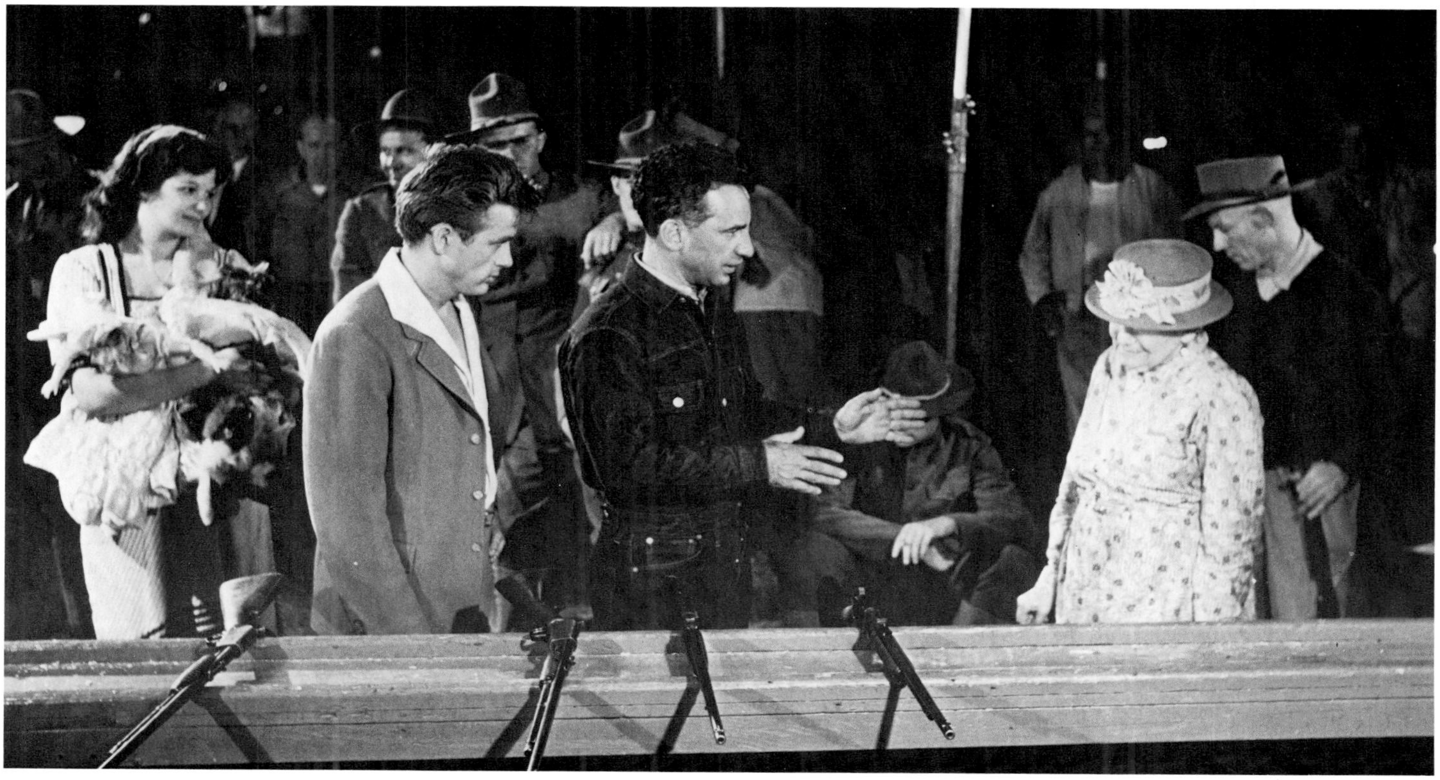

"As I look around, I see
a complete carnival set-up: a huge Ferris wheel,
a merry-go-round, a shooting gallery, a side-show,
various games of chance and stalls with
candied apples, salt water taffee,
and soft drinks."

Warner Bros. Publicity Release
Ted Ashton 7/27/54

"I doubt that Jimmy would ever have got through East of Eden except for an angel on our set. Her name was Julie Harris, and she was goodness itself with Dean, kind and patient and everlastingly sympathetic."

Elia Kazan

To everyone's amusement, James Dean tries to light his cigar on a Ferris wheel lightbulb.

....Roll!

"I came to Hollywood to act, not to charm society. The objective artist has always been misunderstood."

James Dean
Warner Bros.
Publicity Release
Carl Combs: 3/9/55

"So Gadge (Kazan) endured the slouchings, the eye-poppings, the mutterings and all the wilful eccentricities...He said to me one morning...'Bear with me, Ray, I'm getting solid Gold!' "

Raymond Massey

Richard Davalos (foreground), Julie Harris and James Dean (background) await Raymond Massey's entrance into the house for the famous "birthday party" scene.

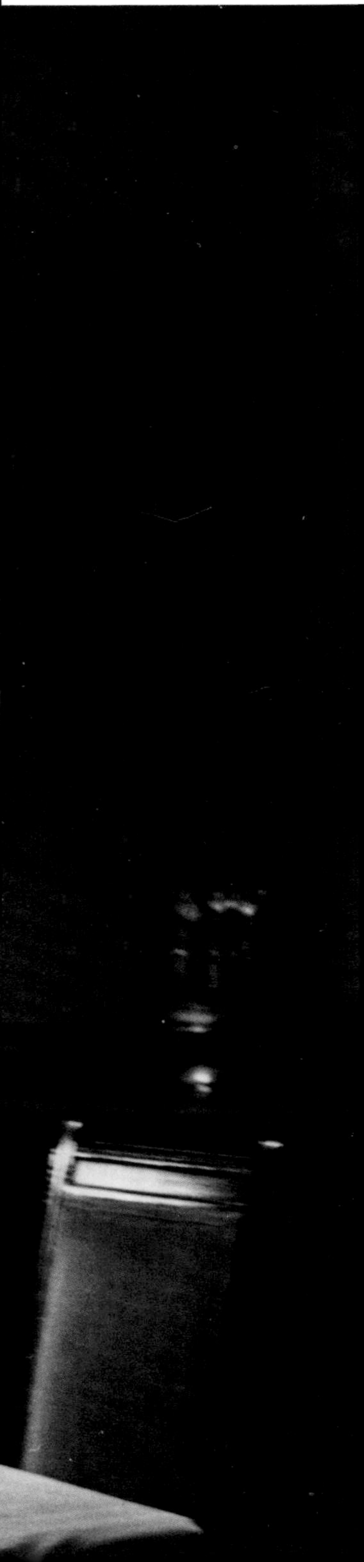

"I couldn't remember ever having seen a young man with such power, so many facets of expression, so much sheer invention as this actor."

Hedda Hopper

"Acting is the most logical way for people's neuroses to express themselves."

James Dean

A jealous Aron (Richard Davalos) "pulls" Abra (Julie Harris) away from Cal (James Dean) in the backyard of the Trask home on Stage 6 at Warner Bros. Studio.

In a scene at Kate's brothel, cut from the film, Ann (Lois Smith) wraps her legs around Cal (James Dean) just after he has "introduced" Aron to their mother (Jo Van Fleet).

In a rehearsal for the climax of the film,
Elia Kazan shows Raymond Massey how to collapse
from a stroke into James Dean's arms.

WESTERN UNION

W. P. MARSHALL, PRESIDENT

1220

SYMBOLS
DL=Day Letter
NL=Night Letter
LT=Int'l Letter Telegram
VLT=Int'l Victory Ltr.

...SS OF SERVICE
...is is a full-rate ...gram or Cable... unless its de... ...ed character is in... ...ted by a suitable ...bol above or pre... ...ing the address.

...iling time shown in the date line on telegrams and day letters is STANDARD TIME at point of origin. Time of receipt is STANDARD TIME at point of destination

NEW YORK NY MARCH 10, 1955.

...-1. JL TO TRILLING AND BLUMENSTOCK ------ OPENING OF EAST OF EDEN ...AS TREMENDOUS. REVIEWS EXCELLENT. AUDIENCE ENTHRALLED. HARD TO FIND WORDS ...O DESCRIBE THIS AMAZING PICTURE.] JL-TRILLING-BLUMENSTOCK

SCHNEIDER TO JL ------- BATTLE CRY WEDNESDAY PARAMOUNT NEW YORK 2250. NEW YORK CONFIDENTIAL VICTORIA 1556.] JL-TRILLING-BLUMENSTOCK

NORTON TO MUELLER ------ YOUR WIRE RECEIVED WILL TAKE PROMPT ACTION TO SECURE PROPER EQUIPMENT AND COMPLETE COOPERATION FOR GRAHAM. REGARDS.] MUELLER

March 16, 1955

Mr. Elia Kazan,
Forrest Theater,
Philadelphia, Pa.

Dear Gadge:

Harry Mayer sent me the reviews and has told me how won... derfully well the show was received in Philly...apparen... another big, big smash for you when it arrives in New York.

Equally as good news is the excellent reception EDEN has been receiving in these few early release dates -- criti... cally as well as commercially. I thought this week's TI... magazine review was unusually good, if you will overlook some of its snide asides. Opened today LA Egyptian and Paramount Downtown and at 4:00PM the figures were as strong as BATTLE CRY -- our biggest grossing picture in years and years. You always knew EDEN had quality but you were concerned about it being "box office"; obviously now it's all of that.

That's all, know you are up to your neck in work and sweat...keep making them good in all directions.

Love from the bunch.

As ever,

Steve Trilling

PS
Mort Blumenstock said he would forward you a set of the local reviews first thing tomorrow.

1256 (7/50)

$

CHECK

ACCOUNTING INFORMATION

TIME FILED

...e account of Michael Todd Company, Inc.

WESTERN UNION
INTERNATIONAL COMMUNICATIONS
CABLEGRAM

W. P. MARSHALL, PRESIDENT

...ESIRED

...l check class of ser... ...otherwise the cable... ...l be transmitted ...t full rates.

...following message subject to the conditions, rules and regulations of The Western Union Telegraph Company set forth in its tariffs on file with the Federal Communications Commission:

Feb. 10 1955

TO OBTAIN FAST AND ACCURATE SERVICE INSERT Via W.U. Cables

To Mr. Elia Kazan Via
167 East 74th St. NYC

Dear Gadge:

This is a fan letter. I saw East of Eden last night and after I recovered from the impact and was walking away from the projection room, I attempted to analyze why I was so spellbound. Most audiences don't do that. They just react to a picture good or bad and let it go at that and want no reasons. But not so with me. I had to find out why I was so moved. First, the direction and casting call for new adjectives. The use of the camera results in by far the best use of CinemaScope to date or for many dates to come. The composition will set a whole new method and technique for CinemaScope. I think that 20th Century Fox should give you a substantial piece of their company for what you have done to make CinemaScope come of age. As I was still under the spell of the picture I was walking up Broadway and passed the Astor Theatre and saw the billing for East of Eden and noticed the words around the name, James Dean, to the effect that this is a very big, special star coming up. I thought what a pity that the Warner masterminds are attempting to deprive the public of finding and making this star themselves. And being the presumptuous guy I am, I am sending a copy of this wire to Jack Warner. I don't feel that anything could stop this guy Dean from being a star although such pre-labels have stopped other potentials. In this case I don't think this could happen, but it is too bad to spoil the unconsicous genius's, the public's fun. When

1256 (7/50)

$

CHECK

ACCOUNTING INFORMATION

TIME FILED

...UNION
...MUNICATIONS
...GRAM

W. P. MARSHALL, PRESIDENT

...tions, rules and regulations of The Western Union Telegraph Company set forth in its tariffs on file with the Federal Communications Commission:

19

TO OBTAIN FAST AND ACCURATE SERVICE INSERT Via W.U. Cables

To Elia Kazan (continued) Via

Jack Warner receives this copy from me he will not only think I am presumptuous but he will know that I am not a constant knocker because I had breakfast with him the morning after A Star is Born premiere and in the face of the tremendous build-up and notices, I not only was not overwhelmed, I was somewhat pessimistic. And this morning I wish I had the power of description to really show my enthusiasm for a project of which I have no direct interest except that I am proud to be associated with the business that made East of Eden, show business and to quote our songwriter friend, of which there is no business like.

Regards,

Mike

cc Mr. Jack Warner

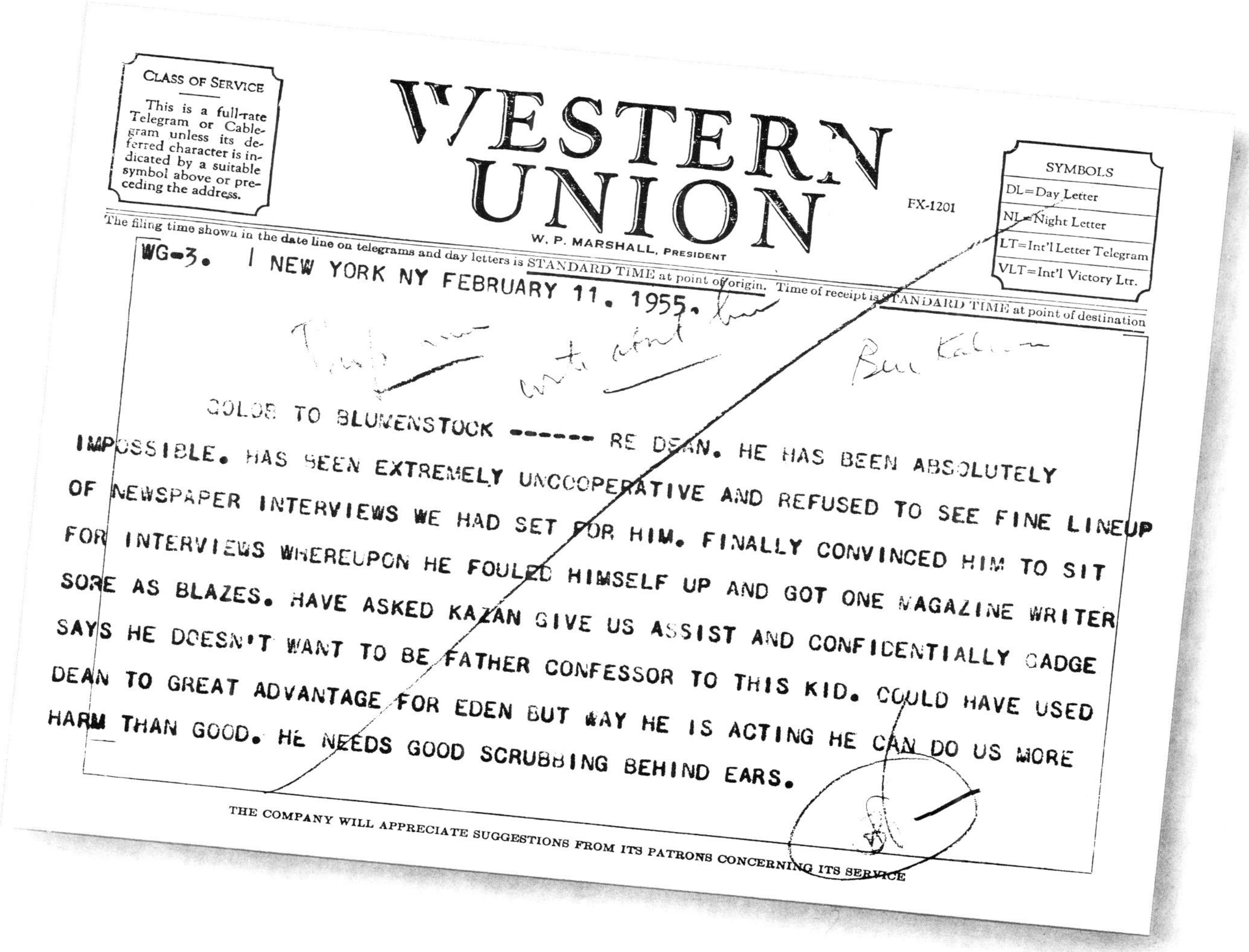

CLASS OF SERVICE

This is a full-rate Telegram or Cablegram unless its deferred character is indicated by a suitable symbol above or preceding the address.

WESTERN UNION

W. P. MARSHALL, PRESIDENT

FX-1201

SYMBOLS
DL=Day Letter
NL=Night Letter
LT=Int'l Letter Telegram
VLT=Int'l Victory Ltr.

The filing time shown in the date line on telegrams and day letters is STANDARD TIME at point of origin. Time of receipt is STANDARD TIME at point of destination

WG-3. I NEW YORK NY FEBRUARY 11. 1955.

COLOR TO BLUMENSTOCK ------ RE DEAN. HE HAS BEEN ABSOLUTELY IMPOSSIBLE. HAS BEEN EXTREMELY UNCOOPERATIVE AND REFUSED TO SEE FINE LINEUP OF NEWSPAPER INTERVIEWS WE HAD SET FOR HIM. FINALLY CONVINCED HIM TO SIT FOR INTERVIEWS WHEREUPON HE FOULED HIMSELF UP AND GOT ONE MAGAZINE WRITER SORE AS BLAZES. HAVE ASKED KAZAN GIVE US ASSIST AND CONFIDENTIALLY GADGE SAYS HE DOESN'T WANT TO BE FATHER CONFESSOR TO THIS KID. COULD HAVE USED DEAN TO GREAT ADVANTAGE FOR EDEN BUT WAY HE IS ACTING HE CAN DO US MORE HARM THAN GOOD. HE NEEDS GOOD SCRUBBING BEHIND EARS.

THE COMPANY WILL APPRECIATE SUGGESTIONS FROM ITS PATRONS CONCERNING ITS SERVICE

"The excitement with which EAST OF EDEN and James Dean were received pleased Warner Bros. immensely and even this telegram (above) to publicity head Mort Blumenstock detailing Dean's difficulties in meeting the press could not dampen their enthusiasm."

FROM: WARNER BROS. STUDIOS BURBANK, CALIF. HO9-1251 CARL COMBS

James Dean, who plays a moody, defiant young man in Warner Bros.' CinemaScope production, "East of Eden," has his own formula for getting into the proper depressed state for each scene. He turns out the lights in his portable dressing room and plays sad music on his record player. Two of his favorites are "Last Spring" and "Heart Wounds" by Grieg.

Elia Kazan is directing and producing "East of Eden" for Warner Bros.

FROM: WARNER BROS. STUDIOS BURBANK, CALIF. HO9-1251

Hollywood is just getting to know James Dean, who was surrounded with the mysterious air of a Greta Garbo during the making of "East of Eden" at Warner Bros. The "I want to be alone" girl had nothing on Dean, who remained very much to himself.

Director-producer Elia Kazan wouldn't permit newspapermen to interview Dean during production. He didn't want anything to interfere with the young actor's concentration in his screen debut.

When not actively engaged in filming with co-stars–Julie Harris, Raymond Massey and Richard Davalos–Dean was likely to spend the time in his dressing room, listening to classical music. It kept him in the mood for his role of Cal, the moody and troublesome brother in "East of Eden."

In reality Dean sincerely likes people. However, giving the best possible performance meant so much to him that he didn't want any distracting influence. He felt there was something of himself in the character. To reveal honestly the things in the role that were of himself as well as the character was a great challenge.

Co-workers at Warner Bros. came to know and like Dean at the completion of the picture, though he still definitely falls into the category of an off-beat character. He even has attended some Hollywood parties and is seen occasionally at night clubs with beautiful actresses.

At one time he was linked romantically with Pier Angeli. He still prefers to date actresses because he is able to talk shop with them.

FROM: WARNER BROS. STUDIOS BURBANK, CALIF. HO9-1251 ASHTON

A Lot of strange things have happened in Hollywood, but none stranger than the case of James Dean, a squint-eyed young man who has become the season's most important new star and has yet to be seen on the screen.

The word has traveled down the line-that-counts—i.e., from executive producer to fervid fan—that Dean has stardom etched all over his dirty leather jacket.

"Apparently," sniffed one movie-maker, "Warner Bros. has discovered uranium."

The discovery by Warner and Director Elia Kazan of Uranium Dean, however, isn't so unusual as the remarkable circumstance that the fans have also discovered him, pressed him to their bountiful bosom, and made him a star without ever having seen him on the motion picture screen.

It's true that his few television appearances, plus a couple of Broadway roles, have helped to lift the veil of complete professional obscurity from the talented young man. But this wouldn't account for the coast-to-coast recognition he is getting as a full-fledged movie star.

"WARNER BROS. PUBLICITY DEPARTMENT CHURNED OUT STORIES FOR THE PRESS ON EVERY FILM THEY MADE. EVEN IN THESE EARLIEST PRESS RELEASES, THE IMAGE OF JAMES DEAN, THE TROUBLED YOUTH/ACTOR BEGINS TO TAKE SHAPE. THESE HOLLYWOOD-HARDENED STUDIO PUBLICISTS REALIZED WARNER BROS. HAD DISCOVERED A UNIQUE TALENT THAT COULDN'T BE DESCRIBED IN OLD-FASHIONED SHOW BIZ PRESS JARGON....AND THE LEGEND BEGINS."

"A great many people, including members of our craft, seem to feel that Jimmy had some sort of secret weapon or magic formula. I do not go along with this. I know that if anyone was ever dedicated to the art of acting, it was Jimmy. He had the greatest power of concentration I have ever encountered. He prepared himself so well in advance for any scene he was playing, that the lines were not simply something he had memorized—they were actually a very real part of him. Before the take of any scene, he would go off by himself for five or ten minutes and think about what he had to do, to the exclusion of everything else. He returned when he felt he was enough in character to shoot the scene."

JIM BACKUS

REBEL WITHOUT A CAUSE

Box 278

TITLE: "REBEL WITHOUT CAUSE" DATE: 3-2-55

JIM

James Dean
Tab Hunter
John Kerr
R. Wagner

JUDY

Debby Reynolds
Natalie Wood
Carol Baker

Girls tested or discussed:

Susan Whitney
Gloria Castillo
Pat Crowley
Kathryn Grant
Cecile Rodgers
Nancy Baker
Georgette Michelle
Laurie Stein
Liza Gaye
Melinda Markey
Sharon Moffatt
Mylee Andreason
Steffanie Sydney
Gigi Perreau

JIM'S FATHER

Tony Ross
Walter Matthau
Bruce Bennett
Harry Townes
Rod Cameron
Vaughn Taylor
Les Tremayne
Glen Gordon
Raymond Burr
Hume Cronyn
Jeff Morrow
Philip Ober
Lee Bowman
Willard Parker
Royal Dano
Dick Foran
Frank Faylen
John Dehner
[illegible handwritten name]

JIM'S MOTHER

Ruth Swanson
Mae Clarke
Peggy Converse
Dorothy Green
Mary Field
Ann Doran
Adrienne Marden
Katherine Warren
Greta Granstedt
Frances Morris
Virginia Christine
Phyllis Stanley
Mary Baer
Vivi Janiss
Benay Venuta
Sylvia Sydney
Natalie Schaefer

JUDY'S FATHER

Brad Dexter
John Griggs
Shepard Strudwick
Whit Conners
Hugh Beaumont
Bruce Bennett
Everett Sloane
Carleton Young
Hayden Rorke
Warner Anderson
John Archer
John Baragrey
Donald Curtis
Bill Hopper
Dick Simmons
Leif Erickson
Doug Kennedy
Hugh Marlowe
Edward Binns
Glen Langden
Richard Denning
Charles Victor

JUDY'S or PLATO'S MOTHER

Jeanette Nolan
Joan Banks
Irene Hervey
Sally Blaine
Marsha Hunt
Erin O'Brien-Moore
Virginia Huston
Ann Dvorak
Rochelle Hudson
Ruth Hussey
Ann Morrison
Dorothy Bruce
Peggy Compton
Arlene Whelan
Maureen Staple
Martha Scott
Evelyn Scott
Evelyn Keyes
Irene Collette
Dorothy Patrick
Evelyn Ankers
Henny Backus

ML-5?5 Rev. 2/53

WARNER BROS. [...]URES, INC.
BURBANK, CALIFORNIA

INTER-OFFICE COMMUNICATION

DATE March 1, 1955

SUBJECT "REBEL WITHOUT A CAUSE"
TESTS - Contd.

-2-

In this light, the love scene in the mansion should be improved.

Actors:

Keeping in mind that whatever known qualities possessed by the actors involved in the test were ignored, in the same way that little attention was paid to makeup or wardrobe, there is only one girl who has shown the capacity to play Judy, and she is Natalie Wood.

At this point, Jeff Silver and Billy Gray are the best candidates for Plato. (Dennis Hopper - only after a test with Jimmy Dean.)

Corey Allen	Doyle Baker
Nick Adams	Butch Cavell
Jack Grinnage	Jerry Olkin
Dennis Hopper	Ken Miller
Frank Mazzola	Bruce Barton
Norma Jean Nelson	Peter Miller
Tony Mazzola	Nancy Baker
Ben Gary	Beverly Long
Steffi Sidney	

[G]loria Castillo has unmistakable talent and sho[...] [a]nd for future young character roles. I do[...] [sh]ows for much beyond character at this [...]

"REBEL WITHOUT A CAUSE"

Ray #821

3/26/55

STAFF & CAST

STAFF

Producer	David Weisbart		709-710
Director	Nick Ray		771-772
Asst.Dir.	Don Page - 4355 Clybourn, N.H.		SU 23150
2nd Asst.Dir.	Robert Farfan - 1752 N.Whitley Ave., Ho.		HO 98454
Script Super.	Howard Hohler - 131 S. Avon St., Burbank		TH 28955
Cameraman	Ernest Haller - 609 N. Doheny Dr., B.H.		CR 47282
Operator	**Bill Shurr - 19526 Ventura Blvd.,Tarzana**		**DI 32708**
Asst.Camera	Stewart Higgs - 11036 Moorpark St., N.H.		SU 21285
Stillman	Floyd McCarty - 9856 Sunland Blvd., Sunland		FL 35352
Art Director	Malcolm Bert - 436 E. Fairview Blvd.,Inglewood		OR 81446
Editor	James Moore - 8862 Wonderland Ave., Ho.		HO 52638
Mixer	Stanley Jones - 4536 Arcola St., N.H.		SU 13754
Prop Man	Herbert Plews - 3119 Valley Heart Blvd.,Bur.		**VICTORIA** 91817
Asst.Prop Man	Robert Turner - 10512 8th Place, Inglewood		PL 51652
Set Dresser	William Wallace - 3100 Clark St., Burbank		TH 62959
Gaffer	Victor Johnson - 350 Mesa Drive, S.M.		EX 56297
Best Boy	Claude Swanner - 10864 Blix, N.H.		SU 11793
Head Grip	Kenneth Taylor - 5809 Lemp, N.H.		SU 24001
Best Boy	George Wilson - 1719 N. Landis, Bur.		TH 64371
Men's Wdbe.	Leon Roberts - 7570½ DeLongpre Ave., Ho.		HO 50011
" "	Henry Field - 424½ N. Ardmore, L.A.		NO 50701
Women's Wdbe.	Marguerite Royce - 704 N. Westmount, W.L.A.		CR 14445
Makeup	Henry Vilardo - 6655 Allott Ave., V.N.		ST 68105
Hairdresser	Tillie Starriett - 5446 Woodman Ave., V.N.		ST 54494

CAST

Jim	James Dean - 1541 Sunset Plaza Dr., Ho.	HO 75191
Jim's Grandmother		
Jim's Father	Jim Backus - 1521 Linda Crest, B.H.	CR 14126
Jim's Mother	Marsha Hunt - 13151 Magnolia Blvd., V.N.	ST 40463
Judy	Natalie Wood - 15036 Valley Vista Blvd., S.O.	ST 99708
Judy's Father	Bill Hopper - 7050 Lasaine, V.N.	DI 21953
Judy's Mother		
Beau		
Plato	Sal Mineo - 4918 Rhodes Ave., N.H.	SU 22375
Buzz	Corey Allen - 10632½ Wilshire Blvd., W.L.A.	GR 83452
Helen	Beverly Long - 9040 Dix St., Ho.	CR 55564
Marsha		
Ginger		
Crunch	Frank Mazzola - 1520 N. Ogden Drive, Ho.	HO 75657
Moose	Jack Simmons -	HO 33952

(CONTINUED)

Mr. J. L. Warner March 31, 1955
Warner Bros. Pictures, Inc.
Burbank, California

Dear Mr. Warner:

We have read the final script dated March 25, for your picture REBEL WITHOUT A CAUSE, and are happy to note the changes and improvements made therein of the first version. As discussed with Mr. McDermid over the telephone there remain certain minor items which we believe need further correction. We list these below.

Page 6: The dialogue beginning "Did you stop to talk to anyone, Judy" still suggests that this sixteen-year old girl has been brought in for soliciting. This objectionable flavor is unacceptable.

Page 28: In this scene of the high-school girls "sneaking a smoke" there should be no suggestion that they are smoking marijuana.

Page 43: If this knife-duel is to be approved it will have to be treated without too much emphasis, and not shown in too much detail. Also, on this page, the action of Buzz kicking Plato when he is down will have to be omitted.

Page 50: In order to avoid any questionable flavor to this scene, we urge that Judy do not actually kiss her father on the lips, but only move towards him with this in mind, which will bring about his reaction. This will omit the actual kiss.

Page 65: We again urge the advisability of not suggesting that these kids in their auto racing are endangering innocent passengers on the highway below.

Page 77: We again urge the importance of not suggesting that these highschool kids consider going in for murder. We feel that this objectionable flavor has not been entirely removed.

Page 85: The dialogue beginning "Have you ever gone with anyone who" and ending "Isn't that awful" is unacceptable as a frank admission to sexual immorality on the part of these high-school pupils.

Page 91: We again suggest avoiding the flavor that these high-school boys are out for murder. Possibly changing Jim's line "We know" would avoid this.

Page 99: It will be absolutely essential that this scene be handled very carefully so that there will be no suggestion of a sex affair between Jim and Judy. Its acceptability will depend entirely on how it will come through in the finished picture. We believe it would help if the scene end in a note of tenderness, omitting the second kiss by Jim.

Page 101: We suggest merely indicating that these high-school boys have tire chains, not showing them flaunting them.

Page 102: We suggest the possibility of not having Plato actually fire his gun on Jim. Jim might wrestle with him and the gun go off.

Page 103: It will be very important when Judy appears that there be nothing about her appearance or actions that suggests that there has been a previous sex affair between her and Jim. The same, of course, applies to Jim's appearance on the previous page.

You understand, of course, that our final judgment will be based on the finished picture.

Cordially yours,

Geoffrey M. Shurlock

Lithograph Billing --- "REBEL WITHOUT A CAUSE" --- August 12, 1955

(NOTE: This credit must be 50%)	WARNER BROS.	50%
	Pictures Presents	5%
No adv. Obligation.	JAMES DEAN	100%
	"REBEL WITHOUT A CAUSE"	100%
	Also Starring	
CONTRACT: Must be 1st fea. on scr. In adv., except 4-col. inches or less.	NATALIE WOOD	40%
	with	
	SAL MINEO	25%
	JIM BACKUS	15%
No adv. obligation.	ANN DORAN	15%
	COREY ALLEN	15%
	WILLIAM HOPPER	15%
		NOTE: Size of fea. players at your discretion.
	in CinemaScope	50%
	and WarnerColor	50%
Writing credit need not appear in group, teaser or ads less than 8 col. inches. See Basic Agrmt. for other exceptions.	Screen Play by Stewart Stern	15%
Producer credit need not appear in group, teaser or ads less than 8 col. inches. See Basic Agrmt. for other exceptions.	Produced by David Weisbart	15%
Director credit need not appear in group, teaser or ads less than 4 column inches. See Basic Agrmt. for other exceptions.	Directed by Nicholas Ray	15%
	A Warner Bros. Picture	5%

R E V I S E D
F I N A L
B I L L I N G

8-12-55

* * *

(AS O.K.'D BY J.L.WARNER)

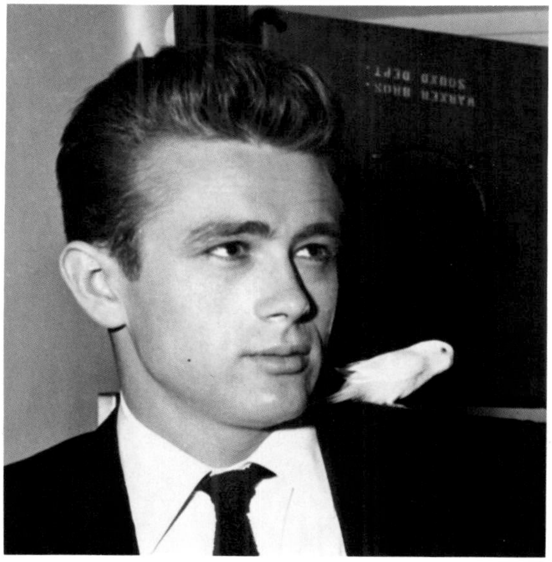

March 30, 1955—*Rebel Without a Cause* begins production. James Dean as Jim Stark—the definitive troubled youth.

"J.D....James Dean!... Juvenile Delinquent!.... Just Dynamite!"

Warner Bros. Newspaper Ad *Rebel without a Cause* —1955

"WELL, THEN, THERE, NOW, WERE YOU HAVING A BALL, DAD?" JIM STARK TO HIS FATHER (JIM BACKUS), AS MOTHER (ANN DORAN), LOOKS UP TO HER FALLEN SON IN REHEARSAL.

PEERING INTO THE CAGED OFFICE THAT HOLDS PLATO (SAL MINEO), JIM STARK ALREADY SHOWS HIS CONCERN FOR THIS FRIGHTENED RABBIT/CHILD.

Director Nicholas Ray observes the first confrontation scene between Jim Stark, his parents, Ray, and Juvenile Police Officer (Edward Platt).

JAMES DEAN EXPRESSES HIS IDEAS TO DIRECTOR NICK RAY FOR THE HIGHLY EMOTIONAL SCENE COMING UP.

Even in rehearsal, James Dean's pent-up energies simmer and seethe....

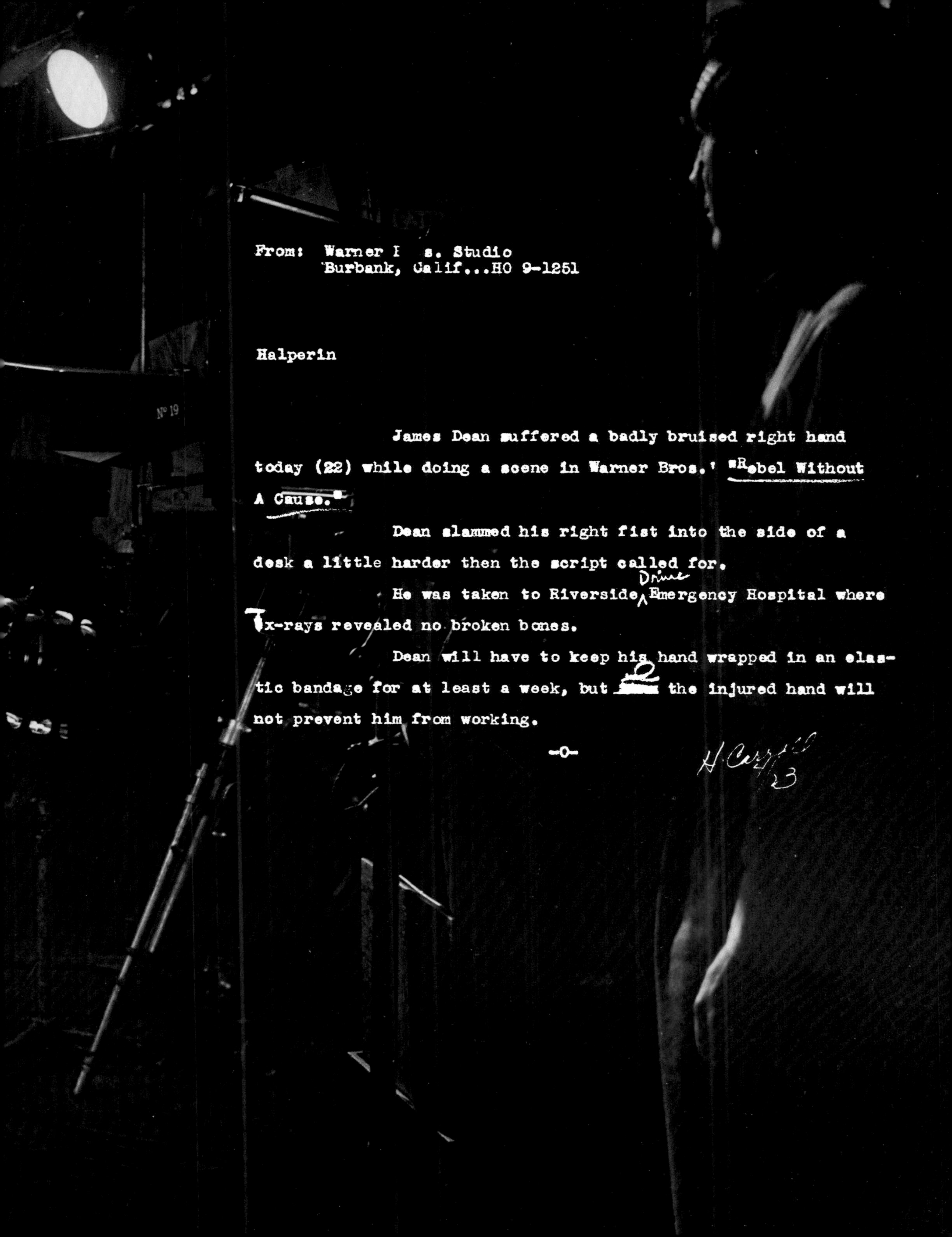

From: Warner B[illegible]s. Studio
Burbank, Calif...HO 9-1251

Halperin

James Dean suffered a badly bruised right hand today (22) while doing a scene in Warner Bros.' "Rebel Without A Cause."

Dean slammed his right fist into the side of a desk a little harder then the script called for.

He was taken to Riverside Drive Emergency Hospital where X-rays revealed no broken bones.

Dean will have to keep his hand wrapped in an elastic bandage for at least a week, but the injured hand will not prevent him from working.

-0-

H. Carroll 4/23

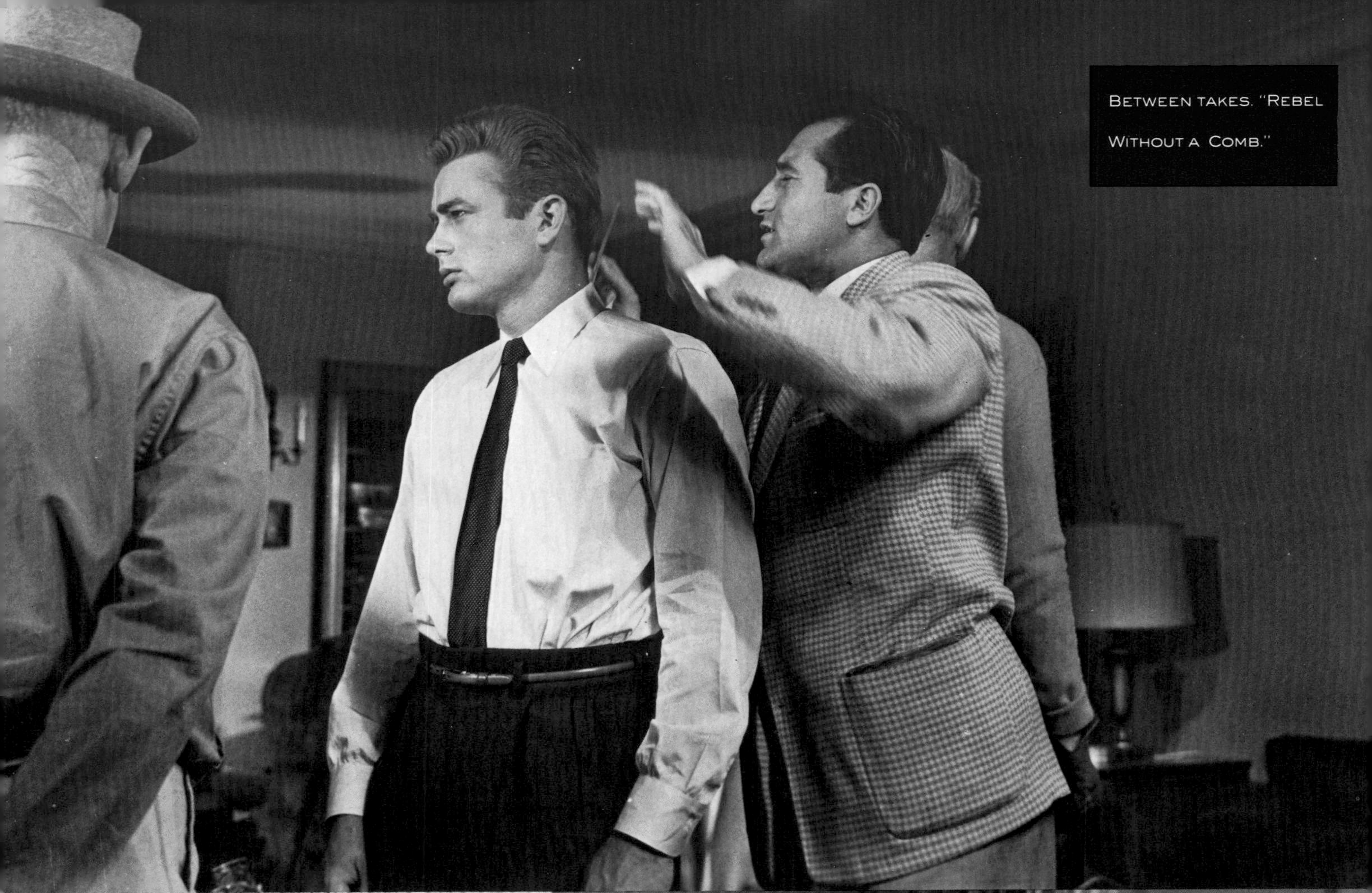

Between takes. "Rebel Without a Comb."

Jim Stark finishes breakfast before his first day at a new school in a new town.

"Even if Jimmy doesn't have a line to speak, I feel he's talking to me. I can tell by the way he looks, the movement of his hands, the slight motion of his facial muscles."

Natalie Wood
Warner Bros. Publicity Release
Halperin: 5/23/55

James Dean rehearses his arrival at "Dawson High School." In the first photograph, Dean is being berated for stepping on the school seal. In the second, Dean looks to Nick Ray for direction. In the third, Producer David Weisbart helps Jimmy with his script.

On the balcony of the Planetarium, James Dean and Sal Mineo look down into the parking lot where the gang waits for them.

DURING REHEARSAL, JAMES DEAN SURPRISES HIS CO-STARS SAL, COREY AND NATALIE, BY ASSUMING A DANSEUR'S POSE, COMPLETE WITH A TIRE-IRON IN HIS HAND.

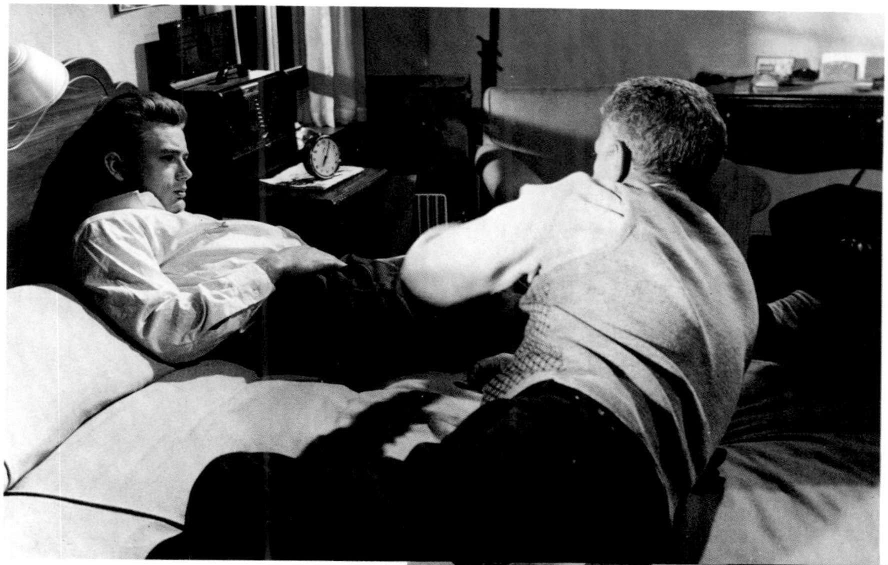

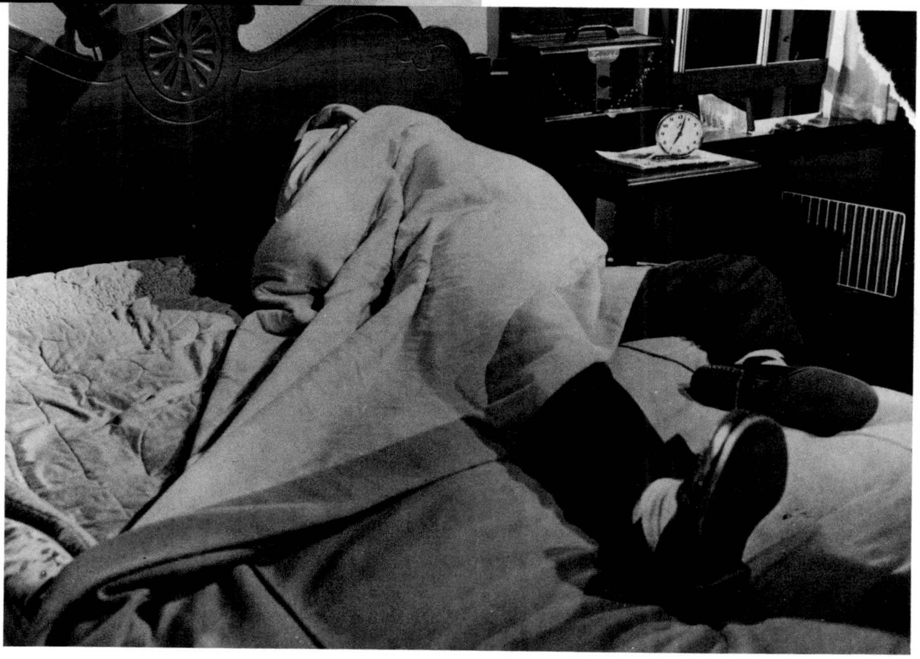

"I've never met anyone with the ability of Dean. He cannot be compared with any actor, present or past. I'm sure he'll bring performances to the screen the likes of which haven't yet been thought of."

Nick Ray
Warner Bros. Publicity Release
Halperin; 5/23/55

"You know, I'll bet you're a real yo-yo."

Judy (Natalie Wood) to Jim (James Dean).
Rebel Without a Cause

ACCIDENT RECORD

[W]ARNER BROS. PICTURES, INC.
(WEST COAST STUDIOS)

REPORT OF "REFERRED" CASES--FOR APRIL 1955 DEPT. TALENT

NAME	EXTENT OF INJURY	CAUSE OF ACCIDENT	STUDIO OR LOCATION	FOREMAN	DOCTOR
Dean, J.	Cont.rt.hand	Struck desk in scene	Studio	Ray	Dr. Hiatt
Tomei, L.	Cont.top head	Struck in fight scene	San Francisco	Tuttle	Dr. Hiatt
Baxley, P.	Lac.rt.palm	Struck in fight scene	Studio	Tuttle	St. Josephs

COPIES TO

_____ DEPARTMENT HEAD
_____ INSURANCE DEPARTMENT
_____ INSURANCE COMPANY
_____ INSURANCE BROKER
_____ FILE

5M 11-53 WL

The hands of Nick Ray direct Jimmy while Corey Allen holds his position for the knife-fight scene.

In rehearsal for the knife-fight ballet.

JAMES DEAN HOLDS COREY ALLEN AT KNIFE-POINT OVER THE EDGE. DENNIS HOPPER AND NICK ADAMS—FROZEN.

Plato (Sal Mineo) greets Jim (James Dean) upon his arrival at the site of the "Chickie Run."

The Fifties.... Fast cars, fast kids, fast times. Jim and Buzz meet for a duel to the death.

The start of the "Chickie Run." Jim asks Judy for the same luck she just gave Buzz.

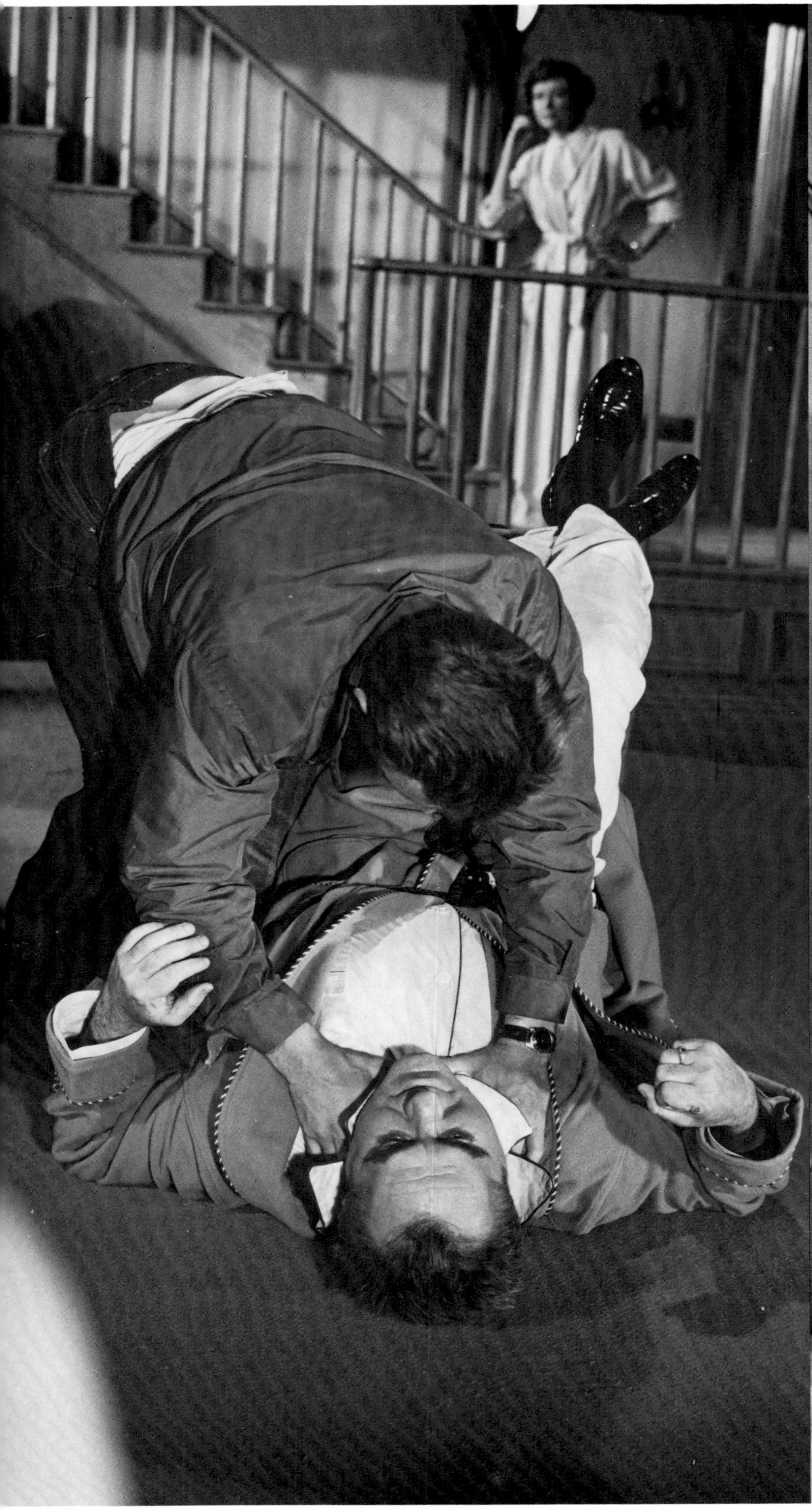

"He knows what he's doing all the time. He pounces on lines and devours them as if they were the substance of life."

Ann Doran Warner Bros. Publicity Release Halperin: 5/23/55

In this photograph, following the "Chickie Run," James Dean and Frank Mazzola trade punches before Dean's entrance into the police station. In the film, they trade only words.

Rehearsing....

James Dean and Natalie Wood, a couple of misunderstood kids, solving their problems on their own.

Playing to the still camera, James Dean sweeps Natalie Wood off her feet.

INSIDE THE MANSION, JIM STARK ASKS PLATO, THE OUTSIDER, FOR THE "PASSWORD."

THREE LOST TEENAGERS
BECOME A FAMILY.

NATALIE LAUGHS....

....JIMMY COLLAPSES....

....AND JIM AND JUDY FALL IN LOVE.

CHASING PLATO—JIM AND JUDY ON THE RUN FROM THE POLICE.

JAMES DEAN...

IN THE NIGHT.

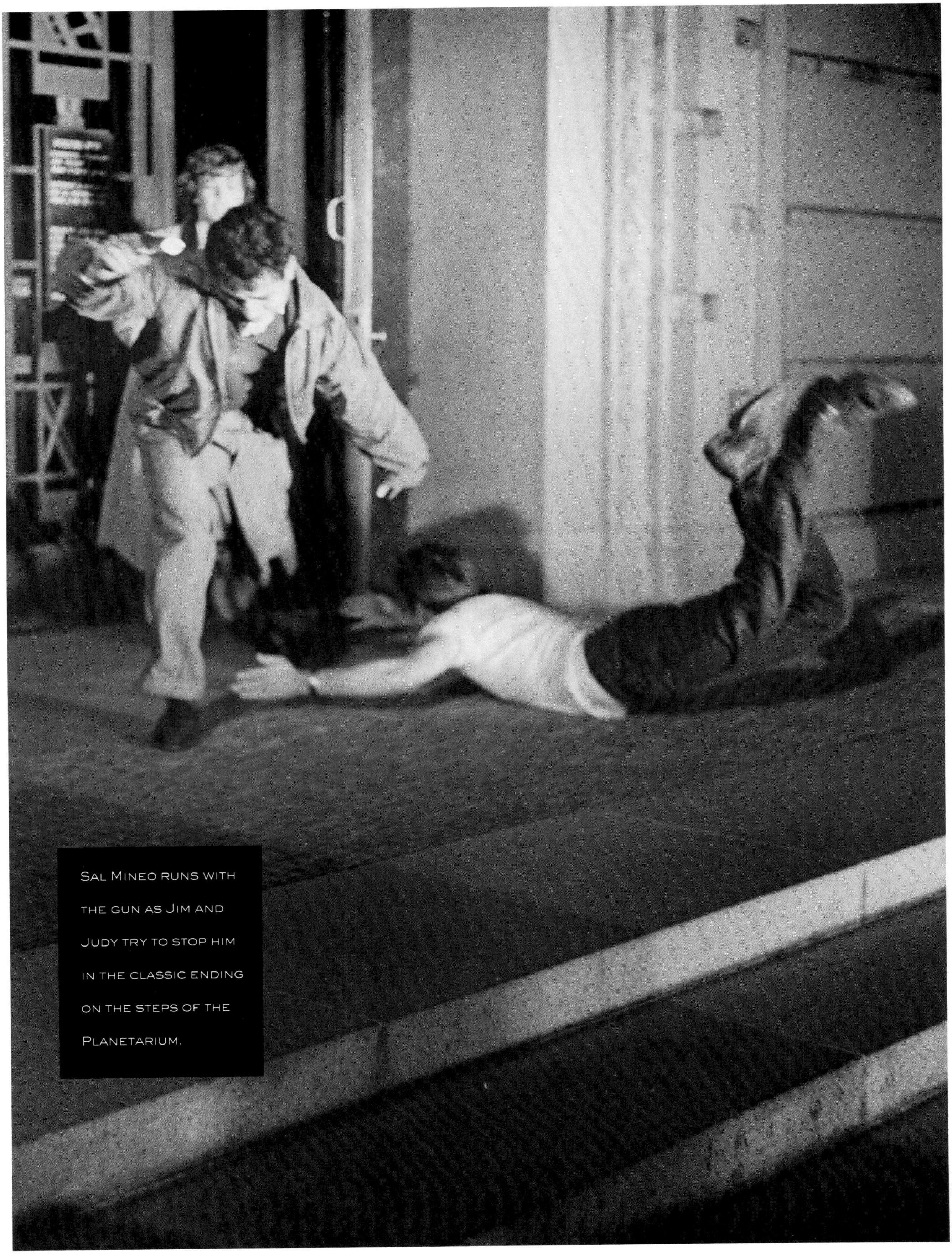

Sal Mineo runs with the gun as Jim and Judy try to stop him in the classic ending on the steps of the Planetarium.

"I'VE GOT THE BULLETS!"

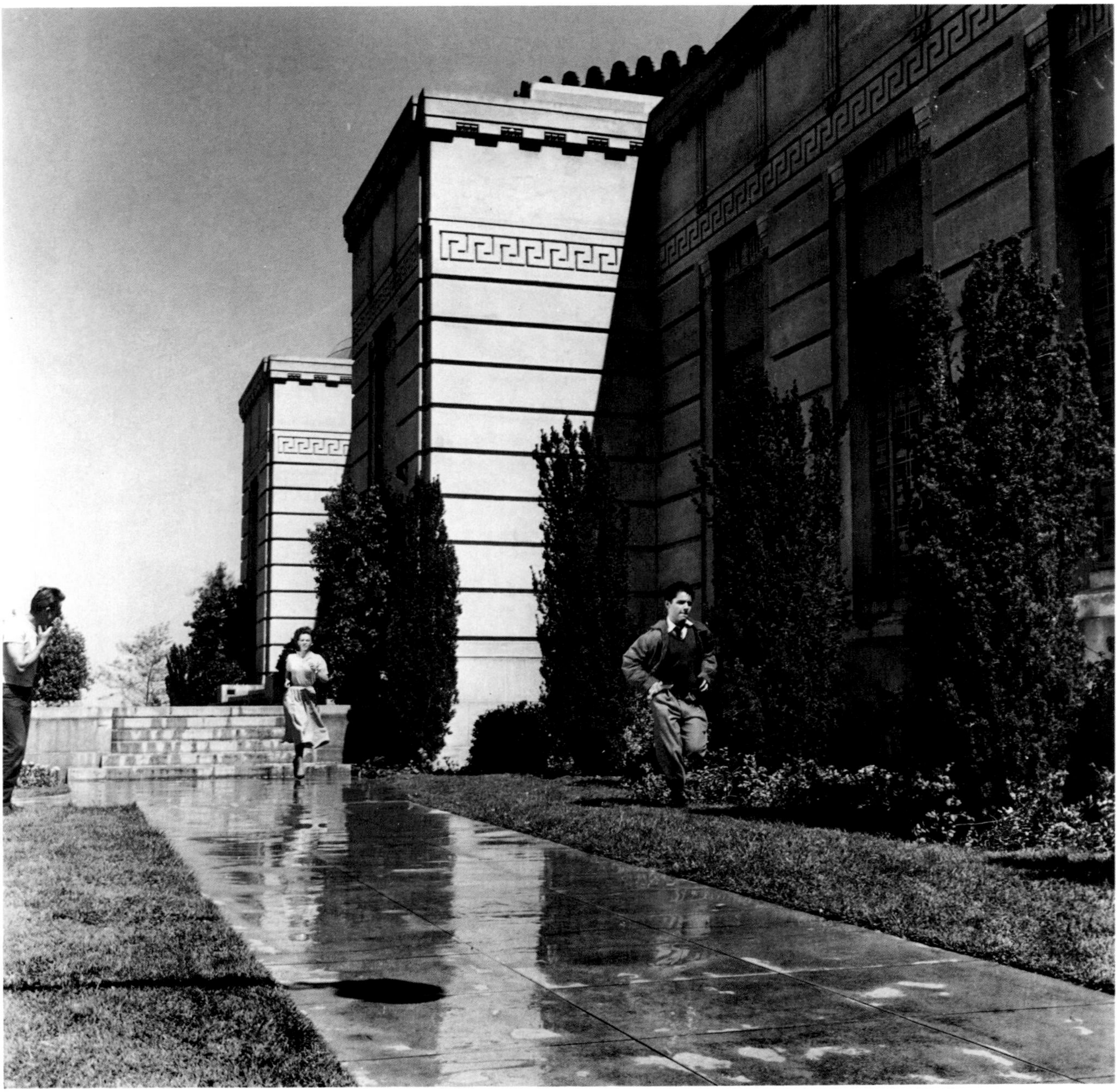

THE ORIGINAL ENDING... DEAN "DIRECTS" SAL MINEO AND NATALIE WOOD IN THE DAYLIGHT RUN TO THE ROOF OF THE PLANETARIUM.

THE ORIGINAL ENDING...

"I'VE GOT....

"....THE BULLETS!"

AGAIN—"I'VE GOT....

....THE BULLETS!"

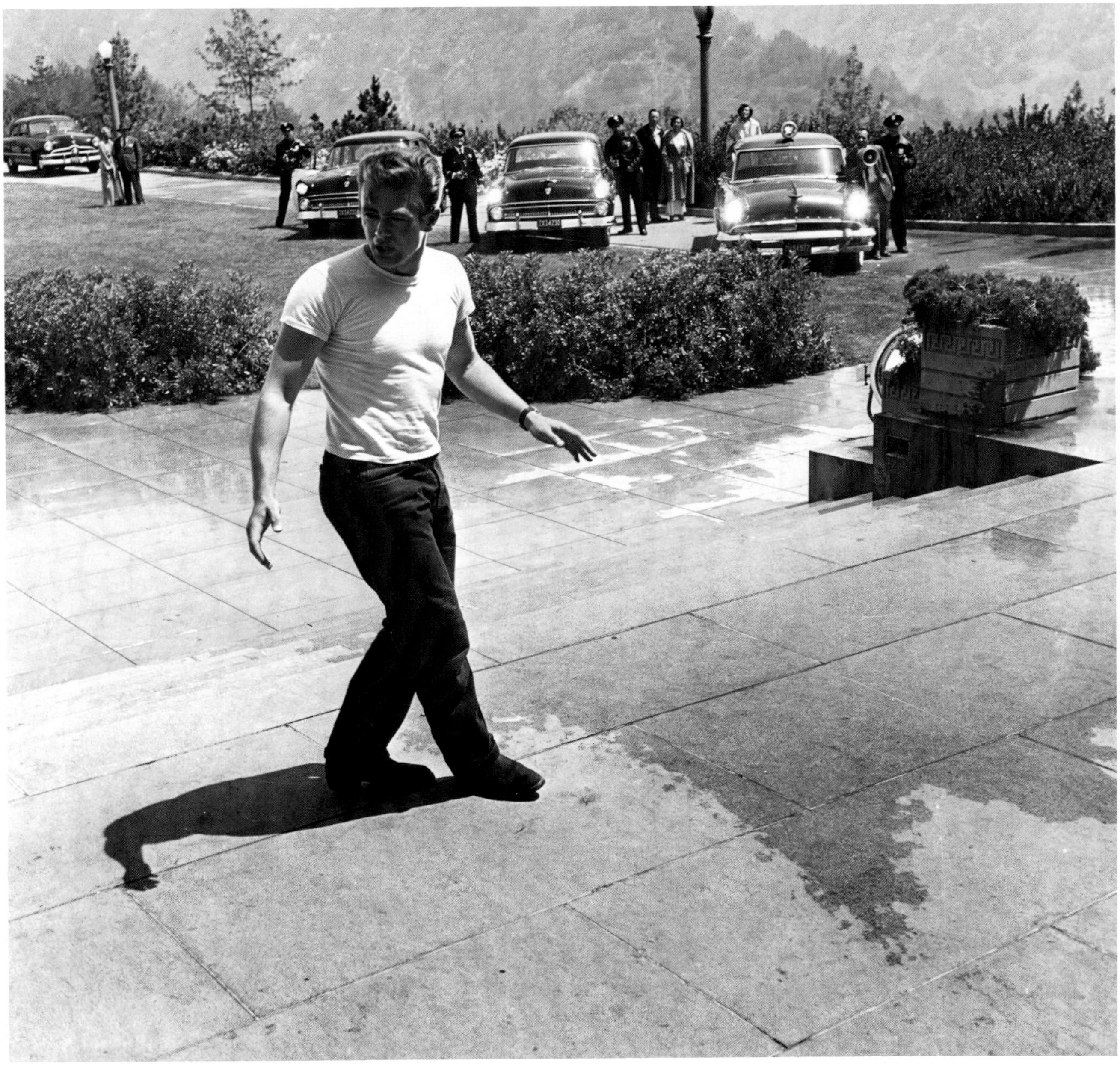

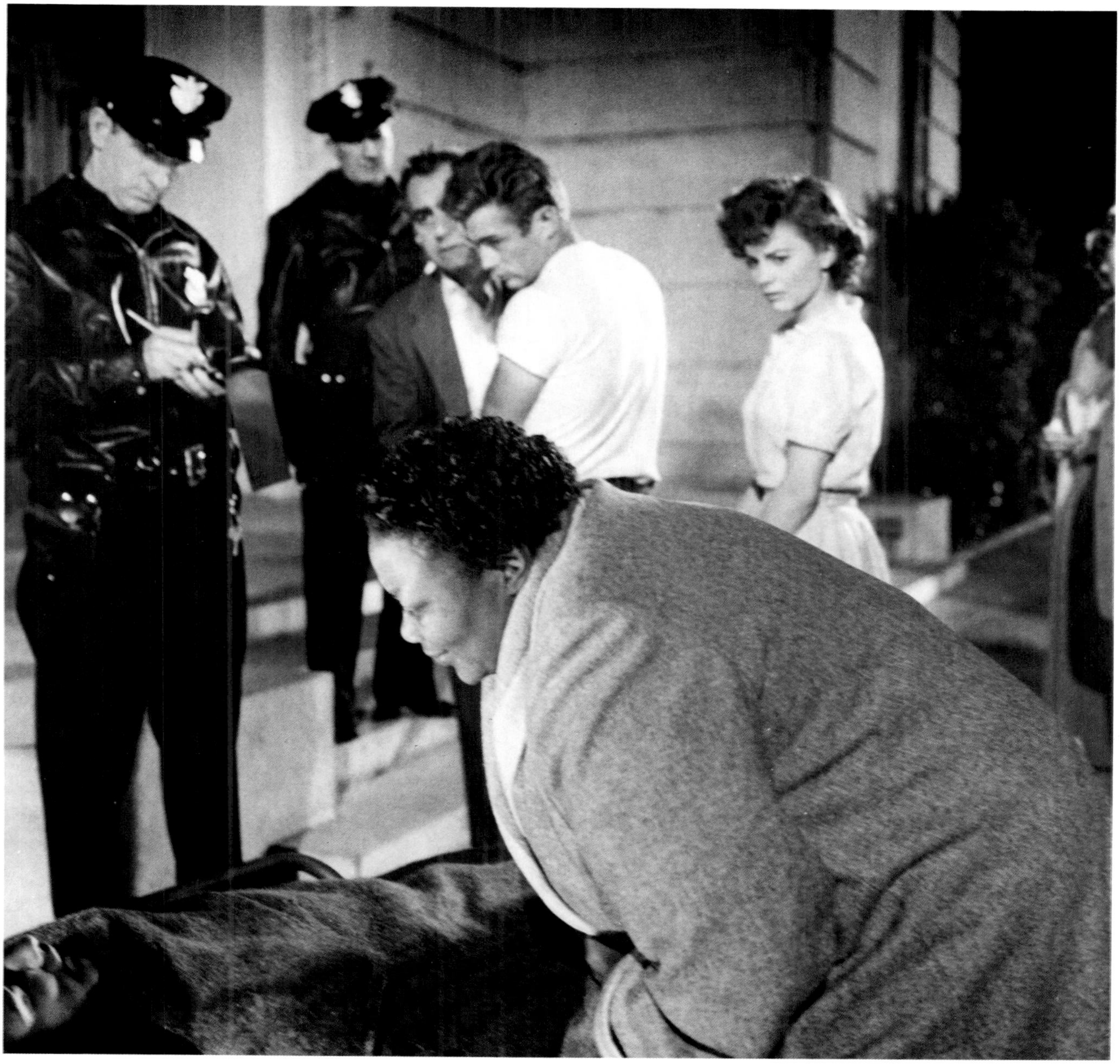

ONE FAMILY DIES AND ANOTHER FAMILY IS REBORN. JAMES DEAN, JIM BACKUS AND NATALIE WOOD WATCH LOUISE BEAVERS TEND THE FALLEN SAL MINEO.

FORM 11

WARNER BROS. PICTURES, INC.
BURBANK, CALIFORNIA

INTER-OFFICE COMMUNICATION

TO MR. J. L. Warner
FROM MR. Nicholas Ray
DATE June 7, 1955
SUBJECT "REBEL WITHOUT A CAUSE"

Dear Jack:

My name is Nick Ray and I just finished making a picture for you called REBEL WITHOUT A CAUSE. I thought maybe you'd forgotten my name because the last time we met any closer than bowing distance was in your office late at night and you wished you'd never met me and I thought you should have felt just the opposite. At that time you threatened with another such meeting if anything else went wrong, and while I know you must have been pissed off at me at least once - and strongly enough to have called another meeting - there hasn't been another such meeting. So either you've forgotten my name or else you have the kind of understanding a director dreams about.

If that's the case, I could use some more (understanding - that is). Here's the problem. We have a lot of footage. (I'm telling you - all right.) Some of it I haven't even seen due to my hours of work, and lack of contact with the cutter. But I know every important frame of it as if it had been printed on my skin, including the out-takes and the unprinted prints. I've seen a couple sequences slapped together for an expediency of one sort or another (with takes in wrong places and the wrong parts of takes in other places, etc., etc.) and yet, because I do know what we have, I come out of the projection room feeling better than the law allows.

Last week, while the cutter was assembling, Dave and I were occupied with post-syncing in order to get Dean off to Texas. The picture was not available and it still isn't completely together.

Yesterday, Dave and I had our first chance to start on our rough out. I'd like us to have enough time to put together a version which I feel will represent the best of the material on hand from which we can all go ahead together into our final version. We would be eliminating those things which you shouldn't have to waste your time with and which we all would find distracting to the overall picture.

I'm not talking about any drawn-out procedure. I can't. Every added day from here on costs me money. For I'm due on another picture immediately and do not feel I can officially report to them. But I think we have a wonderful show, and I would like your first viewing of it to contain as much of its true value as we can get in even a limited but not unreasonable amount of time.

FROM THE OFFICE OF
J. L. WARNER

July 1st, 1955

Dear Steve:

Be sure to instruct Weisbart and Rosenman and all concerned with music on REBEL WITH A CAUSE. As I said last night it is one of the most important factors in the picture especially the last third. Do not let them go "arty" on us.

I sent Benny the following wire:

"SAW FIRST ROUGH CUT OF REBEL WITH A CAUSE LAST NIGHT. THE PICTURE ITSELF IS EXCELLENT. DEAN IS BEYOND COMPREHENSION."

That's how I feel although there are places to make it move about which all of us are aware.

See if the boys can get this ready for a preview before I leave. It is very imperative that they do as I will explain when I see you.

JACK

WARNER BROS.
PICTURES
DISTRIBUTING CORPORATION
1307 S. WABASH AVE. CHICAGO 5, ILL.
PHONE HARRISON 7-6052

OCTOBER 26,1955

Mr A S Howson
New York

Dear Mr Howson

Confirming our telephone conversation of today, the following cuts are to be made in REBEL WITHOUT A CAUSE:

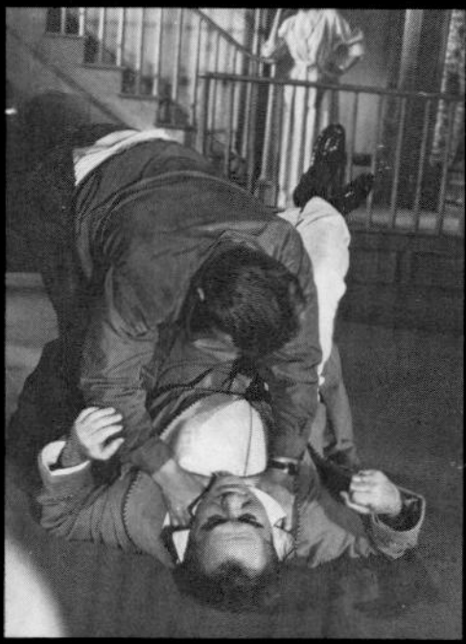

1 - KNIFE FIGHT - CUT ACTUAL FIGHTING TO A MINIMUM

2 - CUT SCENE SHOWING JIM WITH KNIFE AT BUZZ' THROAT

3 - CUT SCENE CHOKING OF FATHER (<u>ACTUAL CHOKING</u>)

Would appreciate hearing from you as soon as possible.

Thanks and kind regards -

Yours very truly,

GL MC. George Lefko.

WARNER BROS. - FIRST NATIONAL PICTURES - WARNER BROS. SHORT SUBJECTS - WARNER PATHE NEWS

CATION

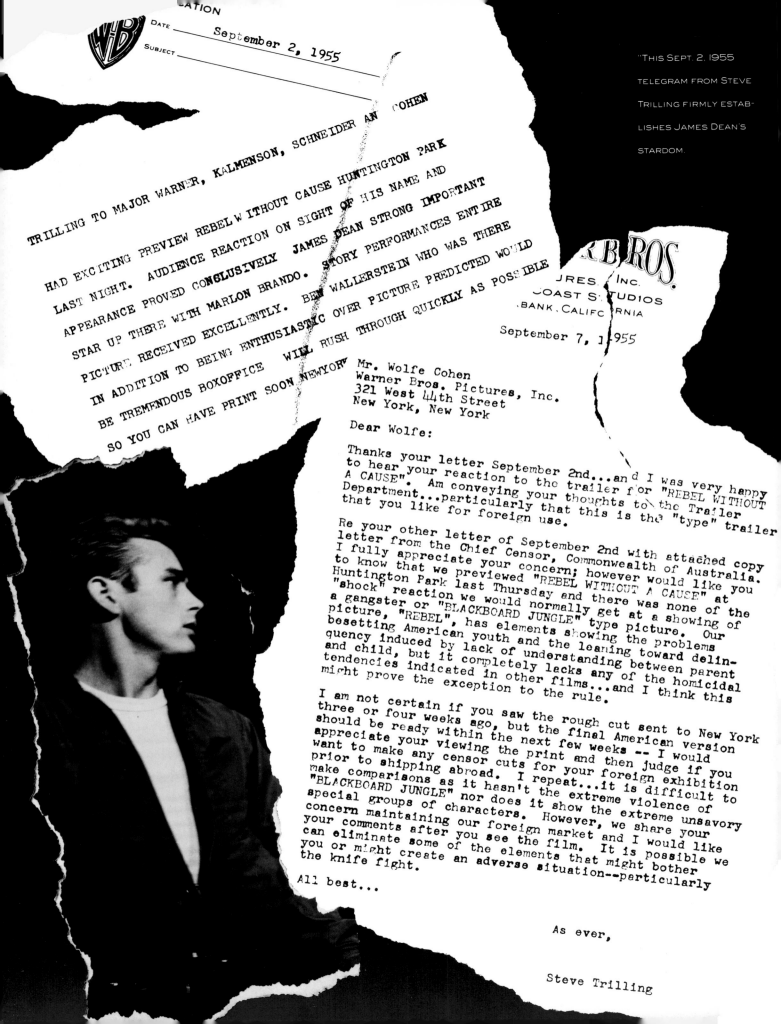

DATE September 2, 1955

SUBJECT

TRILLING TO MAJOR WARNER, KALMENSON, SCHNEIDER AN COHEN

HAD EXCITING PREVIEW REBEL WITHOUT CAUSE HUNTINGTON PARK LAST NIGHT. AUDIENCE REACTION ON SIGHT OF HIS NAME AND APPEARANCE PROVED CONCLUSIVELY JAMES DEAN STRONG IMPORTANT STAR UP THERE WITH MARLON BRANDO. STORY PERFORMANCES ENTIRE PICTURE RECEIVED EXCELLENTLY. BEN WALLERSTEIN WHO WAS THERE IN ADDITION TO BEING ENTHUSIASTIC OVER PICTURE PREDICTED WOULD BE TREMENDOUS BOXOFFICE WILL RUSH THROUGH QUICKLY AS POSSIBLE SO YOU CAN HAVE PRINT SOON NEWYORK

"THIS SEPT. 2, 1955 TELEGRAM FROM STEVE TRILLING FIRMLY ESTABLISHES JAMES DEAN'S STARDOM.

R BROS.
URES, INC.
COAST STUDIOS
BANK, CALIFORNIA

September 7, 1955

Mr. Wolfe Cohen
Warner Bros. Pictures, Inc.
321 West 44th Street
New York, New York

Dear Wolfe:

Thanks your letter September 2nd...and I was very happy to hear your reaction to the trailer for "REBEL WITHOUT A CAUSE". Am conveying your thoughts to the Trailer Department...particularly that this is the "type" trailer that you like for foreign use.

Re your other letter of September 2nd with attached copy letter from the Chief Censor, Commonwealth of Australia. I fully appreciate your concern; however would like you to know that we previewed "REBEL WITHOUT A CAUSE" at Huntington Park last Thursday and there was none of the "shock" reaction we would normally get at a showing of a gangster or "BLACKBOARD JUNGLE" type picture. Our picture, "REBEL", has elements showing the problems besetting American youth and the leaning toward delinquency induced by lack of understanding between parent and child, but it completely lacks any of the homicidal tendencies indicated in other films...and I think this might prove the exception to the rule.

I am not certain if you saw the rough cut sent to New York three or four weeks ago, but the final American version should be ready within the next few weeks -- I would appreciate your viewing the print and then judge if you want to make any censor cuts for your foreign exhibition prior to shipping abroad. I repeat...it is difficult to make comparisons as it hasn't the extreme violence of "BLACKBOARD JUNGLE" nor does it show the extreme unsavory special groups of characters. However, we share your concern maintaining our foreign market and I would like your comments after you see the film. It is possible we can eliminate some of the elements that might bother you or might create an adverse situation--particularly the knife fight.

All best...

As ever,

Steve Trilling

WARNER HOUSE,
WARDOUR STREET,
LONDON, W.I.

November 28th 1955.

REF: ASA/WC/55-84

Mr. Wolfe Cohen,
New York.

Dear Wolfe,

I have received your letter of November 22nd and will attempt to bring you up to date on the REBEL WITHOUT A CAUSE censorship situation.

After very cleverly eliminating the entire knife fight, reducing shots of the girl's excitement before the car race, and making several minor cuts here and there, we got an X certificate for the film.

I objected to this, resubmitted it and asked for an A grading. On Friday I received the Censor's specifications for an A certificate (which are attached) and which I feel are excessive.

In discussing the matter with Goodlatte and Stack, I have come to the conclusion that we should proceed with our X and leave the picture alone. This will cost us twenty or thirty thousand pounds, but to have a picture which makes no sense would cost us more, and I still think we can go over £100,000.

I have just arranged for a booking early in the New Year for the Pavilion -- the West End home of X certificates -- and will probably get a March date on the A.B.C. circuit.

I'm sorry that I allowed Nick Ray to get into this situation, but I did so on the off chance that he could impress Watkins, the Censor, by his sincerity about the moral tone of the film. He cut absolutely no ice with him, however, and in last week's Variety I read some stuff about the censorship problems on the film which could only have come from Ray. I make a very strong point of keeping completely mum with the press on our problems with the Censor. By exposing them we might win a couple of decisions, but in the long run he'd make us sorry we talked, so all our differences are kept strictly between us.

December 5th, 1955

Mr. Wolfe Cohen
Warner Bros. Pictures, Inc.
321 West 44th Street
New York, New York

Dear Wolfe:

Thanks for your letter of December 2nd with the letter from Abeles and the letter he received from the English censor on REBEL WITHOUT A CAUSE.

Abeles did the right thing. To mutilate the film in order to satisfy the Censor for an "A" certificate, would destroy the entire picture. If there are any repercussions on this, will appreciate hearing from you. It's too bad the English censors do not realize that by showing the truth on the screen, they can correct the evils of both parents and children. They should let the pictures mirror life. I am positive that's how it works in our country. I know the results obtained when gangsters were shown in their true light were very enlightening. However, I am sure our pictures will not be the cause of changing English censorship.

Re: Nick Ray, I never have permitted Producers, Directors or Writers to interfere. Unfortunately, Ray happened to be in London and I was under the impression he could be of some help. We will return to our policy of letting Producers, Directors and Writers make the films and we will sell them.

as far as I am concern...

MEANWHILE, FOREIGN CENSORS WERE PROVING MORE DIFFICULT TO PLEASE THAN THEIR AMERICAN COUNTERPARTS. IN THESE EXCHANGES, STEVE TRILLING, ARTHUR ABELES AND JACK L. WARNER DISCUSS THE PROBLEMS IN AUSTRALIA AND ENGLAND.

FROM: WARNER BROS. STUDIOS BURBANK, CALIF. HO9-1251 HALPERIN

(One minute interview with James Dean at a preview of Warner Bros.' "Rebel Without a Cause.")

Since I'm only 24 years old, guess I have as good an insight into this rising generation as any other young man my age. And I've discovered that most young men do not stand like ramrods or talk like Demosthenes. Therefore, when I do play a youth, such as in Warner Bros.' "Rebel Without a Cause," I try to imitate life. The picture deals with the problems of modern youth. It is the romanticized conception of the juvenile that causes much of our trouble with misguided youth nowadays. I think one thing this picture shows that's new is the psychological disproportion of the kids' demands on the parents. Parents are often at fault, but the kids have some work to do, too. But you can't show some faroff idyllic conception of behavior if you want the kids to come and see the picture. You've got to show what it's really like, and try and reach them on their own grounds. You know, a lot of times an older boy, one of the fellows the young ones idolize, can go back to the high school kids and tell them, "Look what happened to me! Why be a punk and get in trouble with the law? Why do these senseless things just for a thrill?" I hope "Rebel Without a Cause" will do something like that. I hope it will remind them that other people have feelings. Perhaps they will say "What do we need all that for?" If a picture is psychologically motivated, if there is truth in the relationship in it, then I think that picture will do good. I firmly believe that "Rebel Without a Cause" is such a picture.

FROM: WARNER BROS. STUDIOS BURBANK, CALIF. HO9-1251 HALPERIN

James Dean has so many off-the-screen activities he says he may have to drop some in order to concentrate on acting.

"After all, acting is my first love," he said at Warner Bros. where he's starring in "Rebel Without a Cause," a youth drama in CinemaScope and WarnerColor.

Dean, an expert bongo player before he came to Hollywood to star in "East of Eden," has added sport car racing, bull fighting, skin diving and motion picture photography to his interests.

"With so many outside pursuits, I'm afraid my acting will suffer," he said. "Only problem is I don't know which to abandon—at least temporarily."

Dean is not only one of the hottest acting talents in Hollywood today, but he's also called one of the best sport car race drivers to compete in Southern California circles in years.

He stunned veteran sport car fans when he tooled his Porsche roadster to victories in the Palm Springs and Bakersfield National Road Races—the only events he's entered so far. He has five trophies for his winning efforts.

Not content with these ventures Dean, who admits he wants to be a film director some day, has purchased more than $2000 worth of motion picture camera equipment with which he expects to produce two-reel short subjects in the near future.

"My contract with Warner Bros. calls for nine pictures in six years. That means I'll have to direct all my energies toward acting," Dean said.

"I think I'll stick with sport car racing and motion picture photography. I already have a sport car and there's no use giving it up. And since I want to be a film director, my motion picture equipment will aid me in that endeavor."

However, Dean is quick to add that actors, like other professional people, need outside hobbies.

"Anyone who dedicates himself to one job soon finds himself in a rut," he said. "I find it refreshing to engage in my avocations. Anyway, if I fail as an actor, I'll have something to fall back on," he added.

"*James* Dean was a dedicated, perfectionist actor. I watched him develop bits of business until they seemed a part of his nature. He asked cowboys to teach him intricate tricks with a rope. He worked himself bleary-eyed with that rope, but if you watch him as Jett Rink doing tricks with that rope in *Giant*, you will see a Texas boy who has been working with a rope all his cotton-pickin' life! I watched him learn how to let his hat fall from his head, watched it do a complete somersault and land, top side up, on the ground in front of him... just the way he wanted it! Every time he did it.

While he was playing Jett Rink, he was inseparable from Jett Rink; he did NOT become Jett Rink, but Jett Rink was his constant companion!"

MERCEDES MCCAMBRIDGE

(*McCambridge, Mercedes* The Quality of Mercy: An Autobiography *Times Books New York 1981*)

CONCOURSE PRODUCTIONS

Photo by Lance Staedler

Mark Rydell

When I set out to make a film about James Dean, I was determined to create a psychological portrait rather than a straight biographical history. I wanted the audience to understand those forces that shaped Jimmy's character and informed his life. Jimmy lost his mother, whom he adored, when he was only nine years old. His father didn't attend the funeral and subsequently rejected his son, sending him to Indiana to grow up with his aunt and uncle. Jimmy had no further contact with his father until he was eighteen. Those brutal and traumatic experiences of abandonment and rejection had a profound effect on his character. They drove him to his highest achievements and ultimately his untimely death. It is my sincere hope that the film documents that journey with compassion, dignity, and respect.

Although I've directed many films, making this one for TNT was particularly intriguing since I had shared so many early acting experiences with Jimmy. We grew up as young actors together in New York in the early fifties. We were both members of the Actor's Studio, and had actually acted opposite one another on William Inge's first teleplay "Glory in the Flowers," starring Hume Cronyn, Jessica Tandy, and featuring Jimmy and myself.

Photo by Doug Hyun

We got to know each other rather well during those years. The experience of knowing him was quite remarkable, partly because of his dedication and commitment to excellence. The joy of connecting with him was palpable. He would often pin you with his eyes and force you to relate to him in an intimate way. He was unpredictable, surprising, and painfully honest. He was quirky, emotionally reticent, seductive, and profoundly sensitive. I admired him a great deal.

Finding an actor to play James Dean was an awesome challenge. As much as I wanted to make a film about his life, I told myself, and the executives at TNT, that if I couldn't find the right actor to play him, I would not go forward with the project. Israel Horovitz had written such an uncompromising and demanding screenplay that without the right actor we had no chance of realizing it. The casting process was complicated by the fact that James Dean was in his early twenties when he reached stardom. There are so few mature talents at that age.

In an exhaustive search, we saw more than five hundred actors before the miracle that is James Franco appeared. He walked in and the search was over. Although only twenty-two, he demonstrated a solidity and wisdom far beyond his years. When we began to discuss the material and do some preliminary work, my heart almost stopped. His understanding of the craft of acting and his dedication and commitment to the project were obvious. And his ability to find the essence of Jimmy without losing himself is a remarkable achievement. His performance is not an imitation but a re-creation and expression of Jimmy's deepest qualities through Franco's own powerful personality. There is a certain "truth" to Franco's acting that reflects his willingness to explore any aspect of Dean's character, no matter how painful that exploration might be. It is amazing how accurate his work is, how fully realized.

The photos on the following pages depict the remarkable feat that Franco--along with the entire cast of the TNT original movie "James Dean"--so beautifully accomplished in shedding light on this Hollywood legend.

People often speculate about whether James Dean would have achieved the status of legend had he not died so unexpectedly. I don't think there is any question about it. When he suffered his untimely death, he had already traveled far along the track to the legendary status he now deservedly enjoys. He was a tortured and driven young artist who wanted to be the best at what he did--and he was.

James Dean was in the motion picture business for only sixteen months--more than forty-five years ago--and yet his image and the memory of him is as powerful today as it was when he first arrived on the scene. Making this film about him was both a privilege and an honor.

"Part of his greatness is that he was so tortured and he was able to tap in to that and show everyone what he experienced through his acting," says Franco (shown here as Dean). "It takes a lot of courage to do that."

Photo by Doug Hyun

Franco as Dean on the streets of Manhattan.

In New York, Dean (Franco) runs his lines during an audition for the Broadway adaptation of *The Immoralist.*

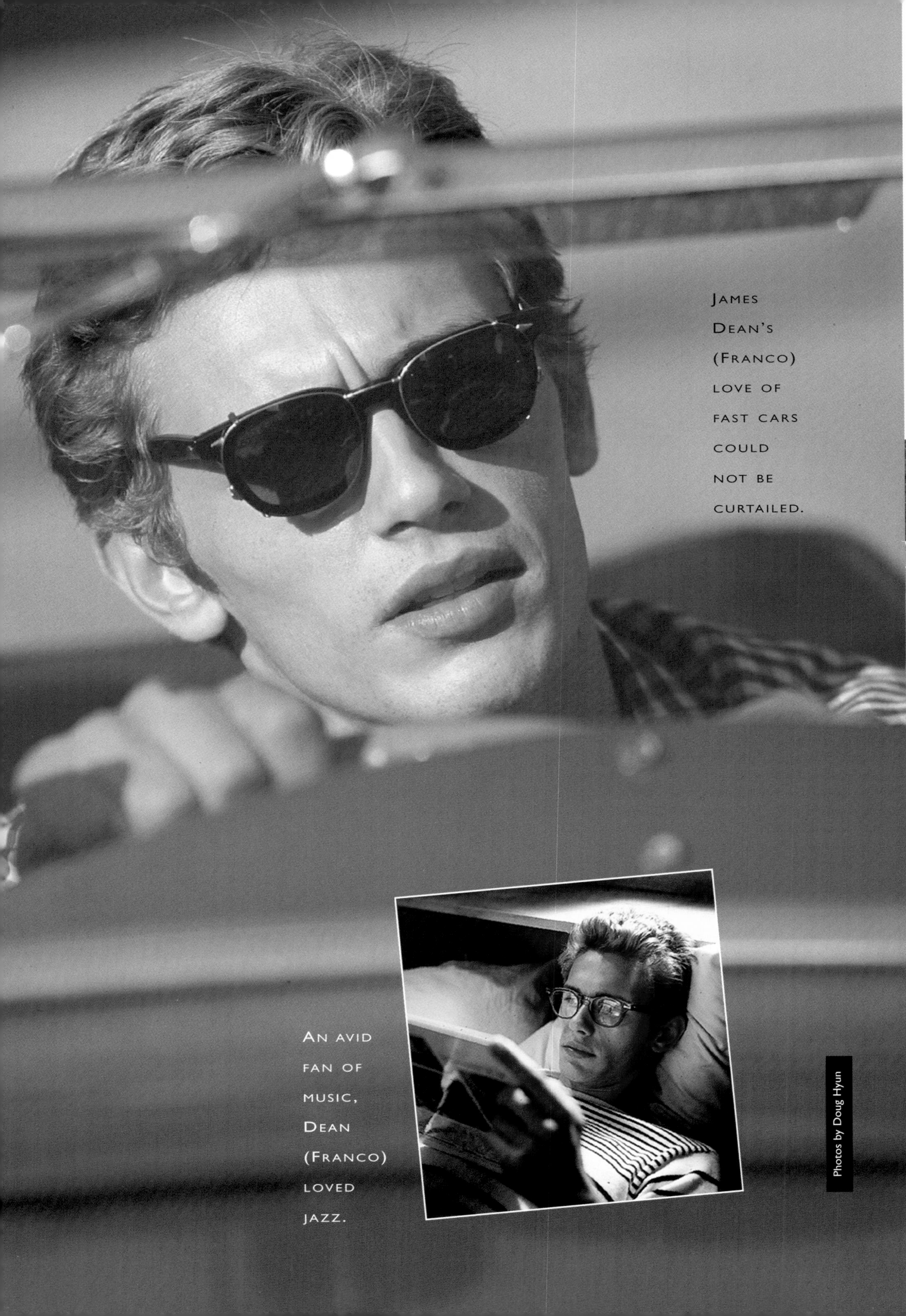

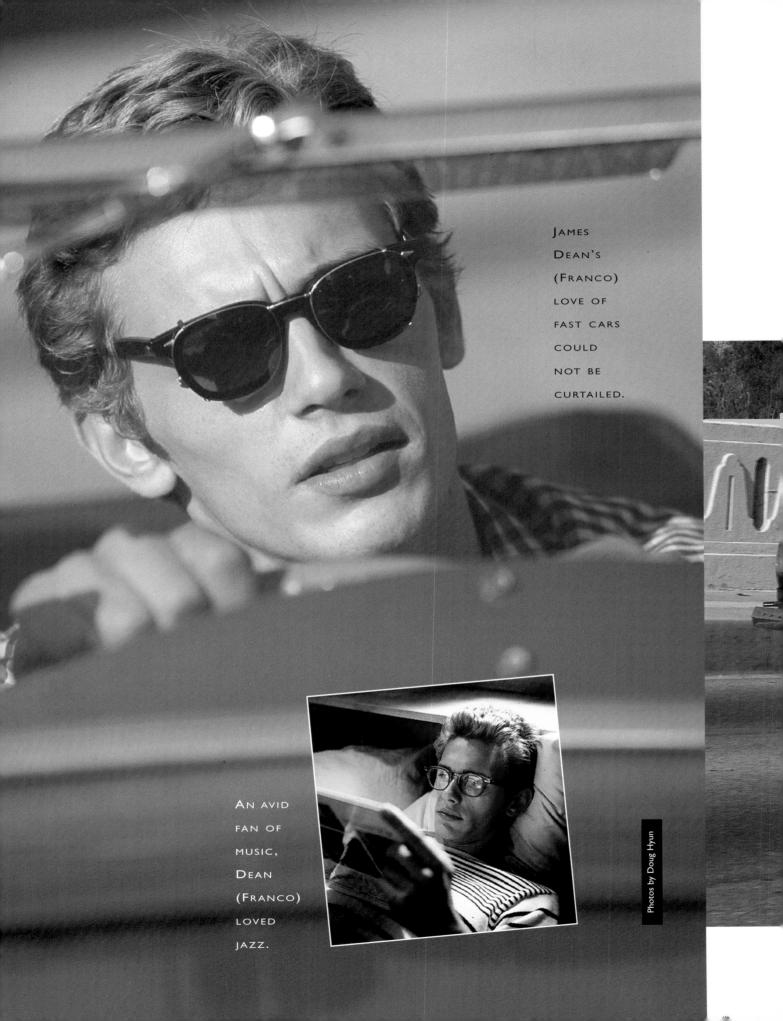

James Dean's (Franco) love of fast cars could not be curtailed.

An avid fan of music, Dean (Franco) loved jazz.

Photos by Doug Hyun

Dean (Franco) on the set of *East of Eden* with costar Julie Harris (Wendy Benson) . . .

. . . and speeding through the streets of Los Angeles.

Photo by Doug Hyun

Photo by Doug Hyun

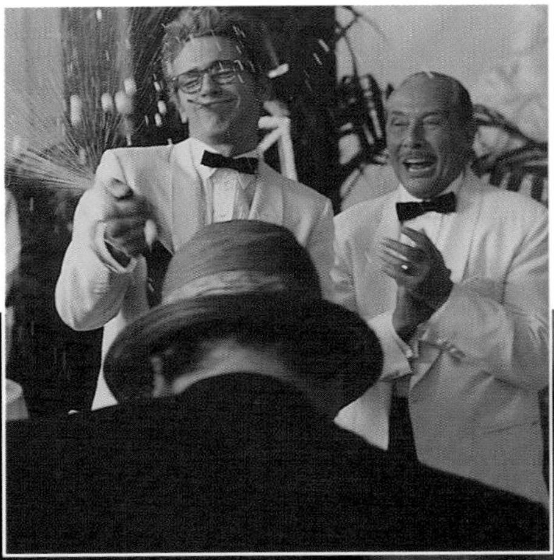

Photo by Doug Hyun

Warner (Rydell) and Dean (Franco) celebrate Dean's million-dollar contract with Warner Bros. Studios.

Photo by Doug Hyun

In his trademark red jacket on the set of *Rebel Without a Cause*.

ON THE SET OF HIS THIRD AND FINAL FILM, *GIANT* . . .

. . . DEAN (FRANCO) EMBODIES THE CHARACTER OF JETT RINK.

Photos by Doug Hyun

Photo by Doug Hyun

Dean (Franco) beside his race car—a Porsche Spyder 550—in which he would end his life.

GIANT

TITLE: "GIANT" DATE: 10/12/53

JORDAN BENEDICT	LESLIE	JETT RINK	LUZ SR.
John Wayne	Jane Wyman	Marlon Brando	Tallulah Bankhead
Gregory Peck	Jenifer Jones	James Whitmore	Judith Anderson
Errol Flynn	Grace Kelly	Robert Mitchum	Mildred Dunneck
Burt Lancaster	Olivia DeHaviland	Charlton Heston	Katherine Empry
Robert Taylor	Ava Gardner	Cornel Wilde	Ann Harding
Jeff Chandler	Susan Hayward	Tony Quinn	Jessica Tandy
Kirk Douglas	Jean Simmons	Steve Cochrane	Frieda Inescourt
Cornel Wilde	Eleanor Parker	Richard Widmark	Sara Hayden
Tyrone Power	Maureen O'Hara	Richard Basehart	Angela Lansbury
Robert Mitchum	Vivian Leigh	George Nader	Doris Packer
Guy Madison	Elizabeth Taylor	Monty Clift	Katherine Warren
Victor Mature	Virginia Mayo	Van Heflin	Agnes Moorhead
Glen Ford	Rita Hayworth	Steve McNally	Nana Bryant
Charlton Heston	Deborah Kerr	Robert Preston	Aline McMahon
Sterling Hayden	Ann Blyth	Jerome Thor	Edith Meiser
Joel McCrea	Jane Greer	John Hodiak	Blanche Yurka
Joe Cotten	Donna Reid	Robert Ryan	Betty Field
Henry Fonda	Audrey Hepburn	Jack Palance	Grace Hartman
Bill Holden	Kathryn Hepburn	John Ireland	Una Merkel
James Stewart	Ann Baxter	Richard Conti	Millie Natwick
Alan Ladd	June Allyson	Howard Duff	Dorothy Stickney
	Gene Tierney		Marglo Gilmord
	Shelley Winters		Margaret Hayes
	Joan Dru		Jessie Royce Landis
	Gloria Grahame		

JORDAN JR.	JUANA	LUZ JR.	VASHTI SAYTH
James Best	Donna Martell	Martha Hyer	Check New York for Names
Paul Burke	Mara Corday	Dawn Adams	
Don Keefer	Yvette Dugay	Nancy Olsen	
Tyler McDuff	Laurette Luez	Piper Laurie	
Chris Drake	Rita Moreno	Vanessa Brown	
Gil Donaldson	Betta St. John	Mary Sinclair	
Jack Kelley	Barbara James Jake	Jane Greer	
Keith Larsen	Anna Marie Albergetti	Gloria Grahame	
Leonard Nimoy	Pier Angeli	Pat Medina	
Richard Long	Abbey Lane	Barbara Britton	
John Bromfield	Mona Freeman	Sheila Connely	
Bill Campbell	Joan Taylor	Gloria De Haven	
Jack Lemmon	Anna Navarro	Jeff Donnell	
Kevin McCarthy	Pilar Del Ray	Peggy Ann Garner	
James Mitchell	Hillary Hall	Lee Grant	
Paul Richards		Julie Harris	
John Barrymore Jr.		Mary Ellen Kay	
Ric Jason		Barbara Ruick	
John Kerr		Eleanor Todd	
Michael Wager		Joan Dru	
Biff Elliot		Joan Taylor	
Dewey Martin		Ruth Hampton	
Tom Drake		Connie Smith	
Douglas Dick			
Gar Moore			
Ron Ronell			
Darryl Hickman			

ML-195 Rev. 2/53

MOTION PICTURE ASSOCIATION
OF AMERICA, INC.
8480 BEVERLY BOULEVARD
HOLLYWOOD 48, CALIFORNIA
WEBSTER 3-7101

ERIC JOHNSTON
PRESIDENT

JOSEPH I. BREEN
VICE PRESIDENT AND
DIRECTOR
PRODUCTION CODE ADMINISTRATION

December 13, 1954

Mr. J. L. Warner
Warner Bros. Pictures, Inc.
4000 W. Olive Avenue
Burbank, California

Dear Mr. Warner:

We have read the estimating script for your proposed production, GIANT, and are happy to report that, with the following exceptions, this material seems to meet the requirements of the Production Code.

Page 19: As presently written, Scene 40 seems excessively sex suggestive. This excess of sex suggestiveness stems from the fact that the scene is played in a bedroom, that our principals are attired in night clothes, that it is their wedding night, and that the entire sequence is played in semi-darkness. We suggest that, if the principals were in a sitting position rather than prone on a bed, and if the room were lighted, much of the excessive sex suggestiveness might be eliminated.

Page 61: The expression "Good Lord" is unacceptable.

Page 64: Dr. Walker's expression "I wish to God" is irreverent, and therefore unacceptable.

Page 111: The word "damn" in Uncle Bawley's dialogue is unacceptable.

Page 126: Jett's use of the word "damn" is unacceptable.

Page 145: Bick's use of the word "damn" is unacceptable.

Page 146: The expression "Madre de Dios" is unacceptable.

cc Henry Ginsberg

noted MG

Noted

Page 156: We assume that you will obtain adequate technical advice regarding the portrayal of the marriage ceremony.

Page 170: Bick's expression "Good Lord" is unacceptable.

Page 183: Watts' expression "Lord" is unacceptable.

Page 194: Jordy's expression "Good Lord" and Bick's expression "Lord" are unacceptable.

Page 199: The expression "Madre Dios" is unacceptable.

Page 202: Jett's use of the word "damn" is unacceptable.

Page 211: The fight sequence, as well as other scenes of physical conflict, must be handled with great care in order that there be no excessive brutality or gruesomeness. Of late, our industry has received severe criticism from many quarters for what has been termed our "sadistic love of brutality for its own sake." We strongly urge you to exercise great restraint in this matter in order that we may belie the charge made against our industry of being exploiters of sadism.

Page 214: Bick's expression "Good Lord" is unacceptable.

You understand, of course, that our final judgment will be based on the finished picture.

Cordially yours,

G. M. Shurlock

Geoffrey M. Shurlock

P. S. We have also read one changed page (218) dated 12/5/54, for this production, and it seems to be acceptable.

FORM 11

COPY

WARNER BROS. PICTURES, INC.
BURBANK, CALIFORNIA

INTER-OFFICE COMMUNICATION

TO MR. HENRY GINSBERG
GIANT PRODUCTIONS
FROM MR. CARL MILLIKEN, JR.

DATE DECEMBER 14, 1954
SUBJECT "GIANT"

CENSORSHIP MEMO

I should explain that the Research Department on this lot is charged with a secondary responsibility; namely, assisting the Legal Department in the examination of scripts with a view to anticipating, if possible, any lawsuits that might arise from our defaming anybody or violating their individual right of privacy. Since Warner Bros. Pictures, Inc. will be a co-defendant in any action brought against an independent producer releasing through Warner Bros., it is our custom to examine the scripts for independent productions in the same way that we would our own.

Edna Ferber's GIANT is a specially worrisome property because it has been accepted, to a large extent, in the public mind as a true document not only of life in Texas but also specifically of the lives of the Kleberg family, which owns and operates the King Ranch, and of Glenn McCarthy, the much publicized Texas oil millionaire. In this connection perhaps we need only to quote from the review of the novel which appeared in the Saturday Review:

> "Despite the disclaimer in the front of the book, the characters in "Giant" will strike many Texans as bearing a remarkable resemblance to actual persons. Some will think that this is actually the story of the King Ranch and Bob Kleberg, and of the Shamrock Hotel and Glenn McCarthy, but on closer examination they will find they are wrong. Very carefully but casually, Miss Ferber brings Bob and Glenn and the Shamrock into her narrative, thus proving beyond a peradventure of a doubt that Glenn McCarthy is Glenn McCarthy himself, not Jett Rink, Bick Benedict is not Bob Kleberg after all, and the little old King Ranch of only a million or so acres is definitely not the giant Reata spread of which Miss Ferber speaks. It is about as difficult to identify the characters and places in "Giant" as it would be to recognize the Washington Monument if it were painted purple."

CENSORSHIP MEMO (Cont. Page 4)

Bick says (Scene 105, Page 49), "My old man brought in Herefords from England and bred 'em with the best we had." Although we have already noted the difference concerning Brahman versus "Oriental" stock, it should be remembered that Robert Kleberg's father was the individual in the King dynasty who began the improvement of the range stock. It was he who brought in Herefords; it was the present Kleberg who brought in the Brahman strain.

Benedict (Scene 55) also mentions that his father built the tremendous ranch home. It was Robert Kleberg I, the father of the present Kleberg, who built the Santa Gertrudis Main House, which is an almost exact replica of the house described in Edna Ferber's novel.

Even the size of the two ranches is almost identical. In the script (Scene 17, Page 8) it is mentioned as being "...around a million acres..." The King Ranch in 1933, according to Fortune Magazine, contained 1,250,000 acres. In a like way, the Benedict ranch is described (Scene 347, Page 150) as the "biggest ranching project in the history of the country." Fortune Magazine is again the authority for the fact that the King Ranch is the world's biggest ranch.

(C) JETT RINK is another controversial character for whom a real-life prototype exists; namely, Glenn McCarthy. Both Jett Rink and Glenn McCarthy are poor Texas boys who made a killing through wildcat oil operations. In the script Bick Benedict is portrayed as selling his ranch oil to a company controlled by Jett Rink. In actual fact, both the King Ranch and Glenn McCarthy (at the time he was first wildcatting in oil) sold their oil to the Humble Oil Company, an independent company which is now a subsidiary of Standard of New Jersey. The most telling resemblance between Jett Rink and Glenn McCarthy, of course, is the ownership of a tremendous new hotel. In Jett Rink's case it is the Conquistador, described in the script (Scene 382, Page 162) as "...a twenty-story hotel...a memorable landmark in the history of our great state..." In actuality the Shamrock Hotel built by Glenn McCarthy was eighteen stories, but even bigger.

WARNER BROS. PICTURES, INC.
BURBANK, CALIFORNIA

COPY

INTER-OFFICE COMMUNICATION

TO MR. HENRY GINSBERG
GIANT PRODUCTIONS
FROM MR. CARL MILLIKEN, JR.

DATE DECEMBER 14, 1954
SUBJECT "GIANT"

CENSORSHIP MEMO (Cont. Page 5)

In addition to ownership of such a hotel, there is even greater danger in the tremendous party which is thrown for invited guests. It will be remembered by the public that McCarthy imported planeloads of Hollywood celebrities and other dignitaries. Jett Rink is shown as doing likewise. Hollywood personalities are mentioned as being in attendance, and (Scene 382, Page 162) Pinky says, "Yeh, they say you have to have 10 million just to get on the guest list," whereupon Whiteside replies, "Why, there's going to be cabinet members from Washington and movie stars singing..." Jane Russell led the Hollywood contingent at McCarthy's party, and Oveta Culp Hobby was on the guest list.

The physical appearance of our sets will be of supreme importance in connection with the hotel which is shown, just as it will be in connection with the Reata Ranch house. To the precise extent that the art director follows the arrangements and decor of the Shamrock Hotel, our personification of Glenn McCarthy in the role of Jett Rink will be made that much more certain. Edna Ferber describes the hotel as being done in blue, whereas the Shamrock is done in green. Other than that her disguise is pretty thin. The extent of our disguise will depend on the sets that are designed.

(D) LUZ BENEDICT, Bick's older sister, has no prototype in real life. To an extent, she might be a composite of Bob Kleberg's mother and a younger sister who was killed in an automobile accident (in much the same way as Luz dies in this story, except that it involved an automobile and not a horse). On the whole, however, this seems to be a fictional character and tends to help the position that we are not personifying the Klebergs.

(E) UNCLE BAWLEY is represented by a real-life member of the Kleberg dynasty. Instead of being an uncle of Bob Kleberg he is a cousin, Caesar Kleberg, and instead of running a northern section of the ranch he actually runs the southernmost section of the King Ranch (the Norias and Sauz divisions). Uncle Bawley of the novel and the script is portrayed as a bachelor, living alone. The description of Uncle Bawley's living arrangements which is contained in the novel is identical with the description

TO: Eric Stacey

FROM: Tom Andre 7-25-55

James Dean was given a call for work (Interior of Truck - Process) on Stage 5 upon his dismissal Friday night, July 22, by both Rusty Meeks and Read Kilgore, second assistant directors, for 8:30 AM makeup, to be ready at 9:00 AM. He was told he would be through possibly by noon and arranged with Bob Hinkle (Texas Talk Coach) to get him a pickup truck to move his residence from 1541 Sunset Playa Drive to a new residence (address unknown) in Sherman Oaks. The truck was to be used after lunch on Saturday.

Saturday morning Dean was not in makeup at 8:30 and Rusty called his (Dean's) message service - HOllywood 7-5191. Meeks was told that Dean had been given a wake-up call at 8:00 and at 8:15. The message service rang through to Dean who told Rusty Meeks he would come right in. When he failed to show up numerous calls were made from 9:30 to 10:15 to his home, with no one answering.

Dean's agent was asked to try and locate him and called in and said that Dean was on his way in to the studio. That the "neighbors" had seen Dean leave. Later the agent was again contacted and went to Dean's Sunset Plaza address. Dean was not there. The agent reported he also contacted Dean's new residence in the valley and that Dean had not been seen there.

At twelve noon the company broke for lunch and it was decided to leave the process equipment in case Dean showed up. Immediately following the lunch break, since Dean had still not appeared, the company moved to the Interior Reata Ranch House on Stage 4.

We obtained the make and license plates number of Dean's new car and I, Tom Andre, asked Mr. Stevens if we should contact Blayney Matthews in an effort to locate Dean. Mr. Stevens felt this should not be done.

At 4:00 PM Rusty Meeks finally contacted Dean, who said that he did not intend to come in to work. He said that when he got up in the morning he was "too tired to work."

TOM ANDRE

T
A
/
b
c

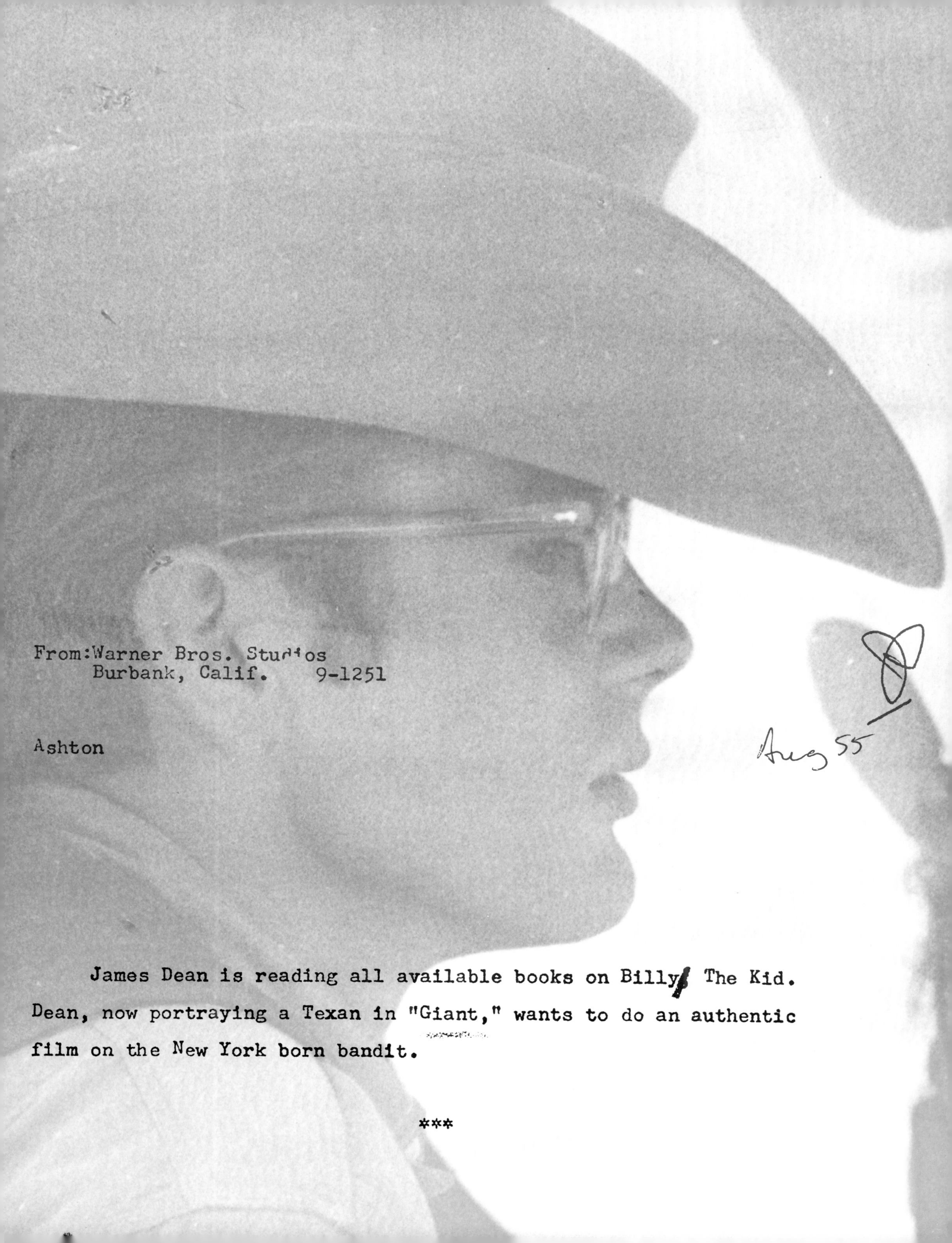

From:Warner Bros. Studios
Burbank, Calif. 9-1251

Ashton

Aug 55

James Dean is reading all available books on Billy The Kid. Dean, now portraying a Texan in "Giant," wants to do an authentic film on the New York born bandit.

***

LITHOGRAPH BILLING — G I A N T — Sept. 12, 1956

Contract	Billing	%
	Warner Bros.	25%
	Pictures Presents	5%
	George Stevens' Production	75%
	G I A N T	100%
CONTRACT: Must be on scr. & in adv. as shown, at percentage shown.	From the novel by Edna Ferber	25% 50%
	Starring	
CONTRACT: Must star or co-star on scr. & in adv. No one may be lgr. or more prominent.	ELIZABETH TAYLOR	75%
CONTRACT: Must star or co-star 2nd to Taylor on scr. & in adv. no less than 50% size of title or word Giant, in event Giant is lgr. than title. No one may be lgr. in lettering or prominence. May fol. title if co-stars do & "Starring" precedes. If any artist photo displayed, his will be too in same rel. size & imp. as co-stars. Need not be in ads 4-col. in. or less if no cast contained therein.	ROCK HUDSON	75%
CONTRACT: Must star or co-star no less 3rd on scr. & in adv., equal size co-stars. No one may be lgr. or more prom. May fol. title if co-stars do & "Starring" precedes. Need not be in ads 4-col.in. or less.	JAMES DEAN	75%
CONTRACT: Must be "Special Billed."	And Presenting CARROLL BAKER	50%
	Also Starring	
(CONTRACT: WITHERS must be "Also Starring" on scr. Size not specified WILLS must be "Also Starring" on scr. & in adv. Need not be in adv. 4-col.in. or less. Size not spec.	JANE WITHERS CHILL WILLS MERCEDES McCAMBRIDGE SAL MINEO	15% to 25%

McCAMBRIDGE must be no less 4th "Also Starring" on scr. & in adv. Need not be in adv. 4-col.in. or less. Size not specified.

MINEO no adv. obligation.

No adv. obligation

with

	DENNIS HOPPER	10%
	JUDITH EVELYN	10%
	PAUL FIX	10%
	Color by	25%
	WarnerColor	50%
WRIT.CRED.must be in adv. in size & style ident.to Dir. or Prod. (except where B.O.val. or contract.oblig. to either gives leeway. Writers' names will be in teaser, trailer & group adv. if Dir. or Prod. credited, unle… either has B.O. val… Need not be in adv. … col. in. or less. … Basic Agrmt. for … exceptions.	Screen …	10%
CONTRACT: Must be… all adv. except … 8-col. in. or less… Size not specified…	Fred Guiol…	15%
Prod. & Dir. credits need not be in group, teaser, or ads less than 8-col. in. See Basic Agrmt. for other exceptions.		
	Presented by Warner Bros.	25%

WARNER BROS. PICTURES, INC.
BURBANK, CALIFORNIA

INTER-OFFICE COMMUNICATION

DATE March 8, 1955

SUBJECT GIANT

J. L. Warner

MR. George Stevens

Dear Jack:

Eric Stacey informs me that you made inquiry of him if GIANT could be made for the budget figure and that he was at a loss to give you information on this matter short of a new script. Unfortunately, this note came to me too late before your departure to give you the following information:

Original budget, plus all added costs, came to $2,912,500. This was $412,500 over our agreed-to $2,500,000 figure. Since this date, no commitment to an expenditure has been made without regard to necessary reduction. Following is the summary of expenditures so far:

Three stars for cast, carried in budget at $350,000, have been pared to $296,000 --

Taylor - $175,000
Hudson - 100,000
Dean - 21,000

Reduction here -- $54,000.

… now OK'd and in work, called for an expenditure of … cost of $192,000. A reduction … reduced …

FROM: WARNER BROS. STUDIOS BURBANK, CALIF. HO9-1251 HALPERIN

James Dean thinks every young actor should have a "Director's Notebook."

"A director's notebook," Dean explains, "is just an ordinary pad, but it has a very definite purpose in the acting profession.

"I use it to take notes on how a director works, how he uses lights, how he gets interesting and intricate camera angles, and just about every technique he employs in the shooting of a motion picture."

Dean first began using the notebook on "East of Eden." He says he took down more than 40 pages of notes on the directing technique of Elia Kazan.

"I hope to use the notes as research material and background data when I make that big move into the field of directing. I know it won't come for a long while, but I'm preparing," Dean says.

While filming Warner Bros.' "Rebel Without a Cause," Cinema-Scope-WarnerColor youth drama, Dean used up more than two notebooks observing the operation of Director Nicholas Ray.

"And when I went into George Stevens' production of 'Giant' at Warners, I had another notebook," Dean explains.

"I hope to have a collection of notes on the technique of all of Hollywood's great motion picture directors."

James Dean kept his promise to George Stevens of no automobile racing during the filming of "Giant" at Warner Bros. Studios, but it didn't take him long to enter his first race after competing his role of Jett Rink a few days ago. Dean is entering the races at Salinas this weekend in the Porsche Spider he purchased last week.

FROM: WARNER BROS. STUDIOS BURBANK, CALIF. HO9-1251 ASHTON

James Dean believes the old proverb, "a jack of all trades and a master of none," can be given a modern interpretation. In Dean's opinion,

a man who is a jack of all trades has a better chance of mastering the art of acting.

"An actor should know a little about many things," Dean says. "He must do more than project his own personality on the screen. He should represent a cross section of many phases of life. The best way to succeed in this is to learn as much as possible about people and their pursuits."

Dean, who is currently portraying ranch hand turned oil millionaire in "Giant," George Stevens' production for Warner Bros., concluded, "Any person stagnates if he does not add to his knowledge. I know I feel more alive when I am trying to master something new."

Dean has been practicing what he preaches in a variety of fields. His exploits on the automobile racing tracks were well publicized earlier this year. He won five trophies, though he had never raced before.

He gives intense concentration and dedication to any new interest. For his role of a Texas rancher in "Giant" he was determined to become expert at roping and horseback riding in order to get the feel of the man he was portraying. As a result he's now good enough to contemplate entering a rodeo or two as a fresh challenge.

On the cultural side, between scenes of "Giant" he has been concentrating on sculpting. He already has done busts of Edna Ferber, Elizabeth Taylor and one of himself.

During the past few years his restless curiosity has driven Dean to get acquainted with such varied pursuits as learning how to fight a bull, studying Aztec culture and playing the piano and the bongo drums. He also has learned to play tennis, to sail and has been studying several foreign languages.

Dean has a long list of things he wants to learn. "Some day I want to direct. A director must be a perfectionist and man of wide knowledge," he declared. "That is why I sometimes feel there are too few hours in the day to even begin to learn what I need to know."

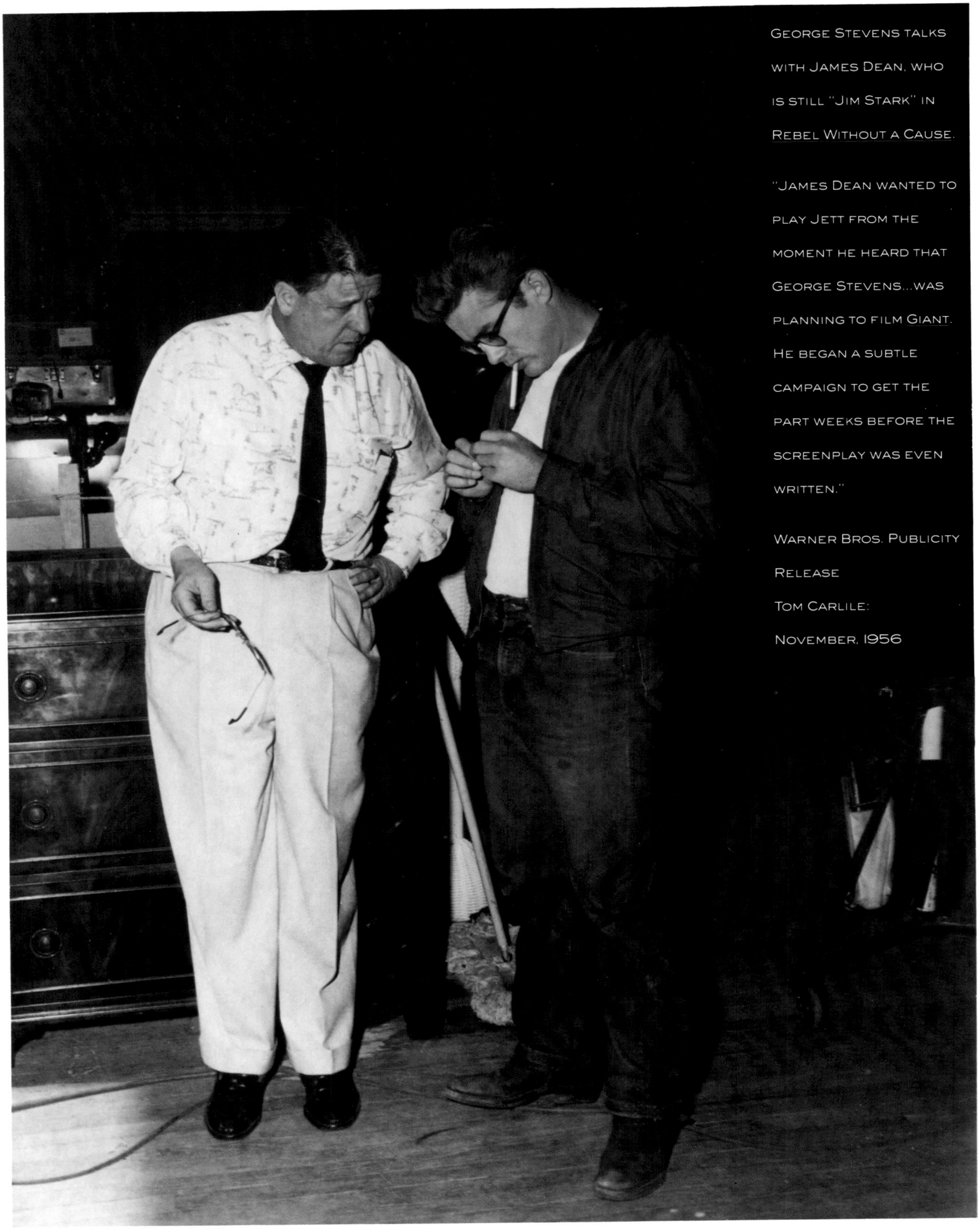

George Stevens talks with James Dean, who is still "Jim Stark" in *Rebel Without a Cause*.

"James Dean wanted to play Jett from the moment he heard that George Stevens...was planning to film *Giant*. He began a subtle campaign to get the part weeks before the screenplay was even written."

Warner Bros. Publicity Release
Tom Carlile:
November, 1956

James Dean with Academy Award-winning art director Boris Leven concentrate on Levin's model of the Little Reata oil derrick, which makes Jett Rink's fortune. Behind them are some of Leven's design sketches for *Giant*.

A rehearsal reading of the script. James Dean is at the top right of the photograph. Clockwise from Dean: Ray Whitley (Watts), Elsa Cardenas (Juana), Mary Ann Edwards (Mrs. Bale Clinch), George Dunne (Verne Decker), Fran Bennett (Judy Benedict), unknown player, Alexander Scourby (Old Polo), Guy Teague (Harper), Chill Wills (Uncle Bawley), Tina Menard (Lupe), Maurice Jara (Dr. Guerra), Carroll Baker (Luz Benedict II), Dennis Hopper (Jordan Benedict III), Robert Nichols (Pinky Snythe), Sheb Wooley (Gabe Target), Victor Millan (Angel Obregon), Charles Watts (Whiteside), and Bob Hinckle, Texas talk coach.

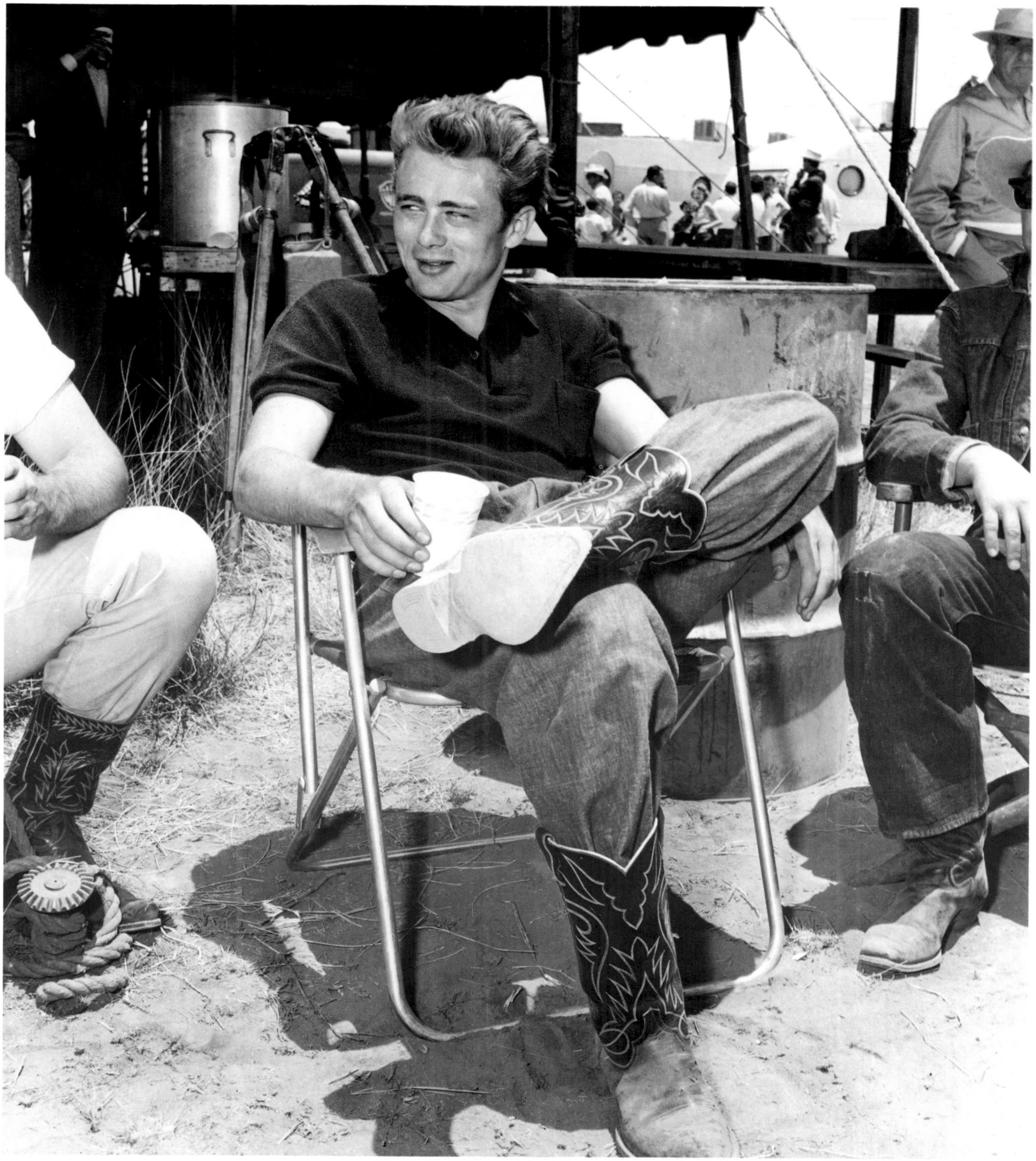

"JIMMY WAS JIMMY— MAYBE IMPOSSIBLE TO REALLY KNOW WELL. BUT WASN'T THAT PART OF HIS FASCINATION AFTER ALL?"

CARROLL BAKER

Jett Rink watches Bick Benedict's (Rock Hudson) arrival at Reata with his new bride Leslie (Elizabeth Taylor).

"...Muh car's broke."

James Dean makes a face.

Up in the air,

planning the action,

George Stevens

tosses down a note to

the crew below while

James Dean observes.

Mercedes McCambridge, Elizabeth Taylor and Rock Hudson watch George Stevens show James Dean how to handle the lariat.

"...HE TRIED TO MAKE JETT A BELIEVABLE PERSON BY LEARNING TO PERFORM THE COWBOY SKILLS THAT MADE HIM A TOP RANCH HAND. JIMMY LEARNED TO ROPE IN A COUPLE OF WEEKS."

GEORGE STEVENS

WARNER BROS. PUBLICITY RELEASE

TOM CARLILE:

NOVEMBER. 1956

"George Stevens... tried to force Jimmy to conform to George's interpretation of the role. Now Jimmy could be led but not driven."

Hedda Hopper

Walking down a road from nowhere—James Dean.

In the original script, Jett Rink was not present at the "Barbecue" celebration, but director George Stevens added his presence on the fringe of the party, alone in a car, watching the festivities.

Mercedes McCambridge and James Dean.

"He had the kind of animal vitality that cannot have escaped the notice of the dry and sequestered figure of Bick's spinster sister, even though she was almost double his age."

Jett Rink: A Profile
Warner Bros. Story Dept. 1954

Jett Rink and Leslie Benedict—together on the Reata Ranch.

TEXAS
22 44

James Dean tells George Stevens how he'd like to play the scene.

....ABANDONED....

On the Reata set at Warner Bros. in Burbank, Jett Rink practices rope tricks and waits for the reading of Luz's will.

"He could do anything he set his mind to...He learned to ride and rope, until he could twirl a lariat as well as Will Rogers."

Hedda Hopper

BETWEEN SCENES,
JAMES DEAN CONTINUES
TO PERFECT HIS ROPE
TRICKS.

IN PREPARATION
FOR A TAKE,
JAMES DEAN BECOMES
NAPOLEON BONAPARTE
TO BECOME JETT RINK.

JETT RINK—ALONE IN A CROWD.

In the actual film, the shy Jett Rink passes by Leslie Benedict and exits without a word.

Following Luz's funeral, this meeting between Jett and Leslie, does not occur in the finished film.

Jett Rink hangs
his hat on a post
and prepares to walk
Little Reata, the piece
of land willed him by
Luz Benedict.

EXTERIOR JETT RINK'S PLACE (DAY) 50M LONG SHOT.

JETT ENTERS CAMERA LEFT—GOES TO WINDMILL—CLIMBS IT—

LOOKS—SITS DOWN. CAMERA REPORT: GIANT

SCENE 149

FINDING THE MANMADE SHADE A WELCOME RELIEF FROM THE HOT TEXAS SUN, JAMES DEAN AND HENRY GINSBERG SPEND A FEW MINUTES TOGETHER BEFORE THE CAMERA ROLLS AGAIN.

THE MAIN GATE AT LITTLE REATA.

Right now, on Little Reata, water is the only thing that pours from the earth for Jett Rink and his dog.

Even under the hot Texas sun, the Hollywood production crew has to add more light in order to film Leslie Benedict's arrival at Little Reata. An umbrella protects the camera from direct sunlight, but James Dean has to play the scene in a heavy wool jacket, as if it was a chilly Texas morning.

Jett follows Leslie
Benedict to his shack
where he prepares tea
for the only woman
he'll ever really love.

Rehearsing one of the most famous photographs in movie history—"The Crucifixion of James Dean".

While Leslie waits for her tea, Jett fortifies his courage.

JAMES DEAN—THE ACTOR PREPARES.

In this sequence of photographs, George Stevens shows two oil-riggers how to carry the pipe while James Dean watches closely.

WHILE THE OIL DERRICK IS BEING READIED—SEATED LEFT TO RIGHT:
CINEMATOGRAPHER BILL MELLOR (WEARING PLAID SHIRT), 2ND-UNIT DIRECTOR FRED GUIOL,
JAMES DEAN AND GEORGE STEVENS OUTSIDE MARFA, TEXAS.

A GUSHER COMES IN AND BLACK GOLD REACHES FOR THE WEST TEXAS SKY.

Before the next scene, James Dean applies his own "makeup"...not a pleasant experience.

Director George Stevens leans against a column and listens to a rehearsal of the fight between Bick Benedict and Jett Rink. In this sequence, Rock Hudson hits first... second......and third....

....but James Dean hits last.

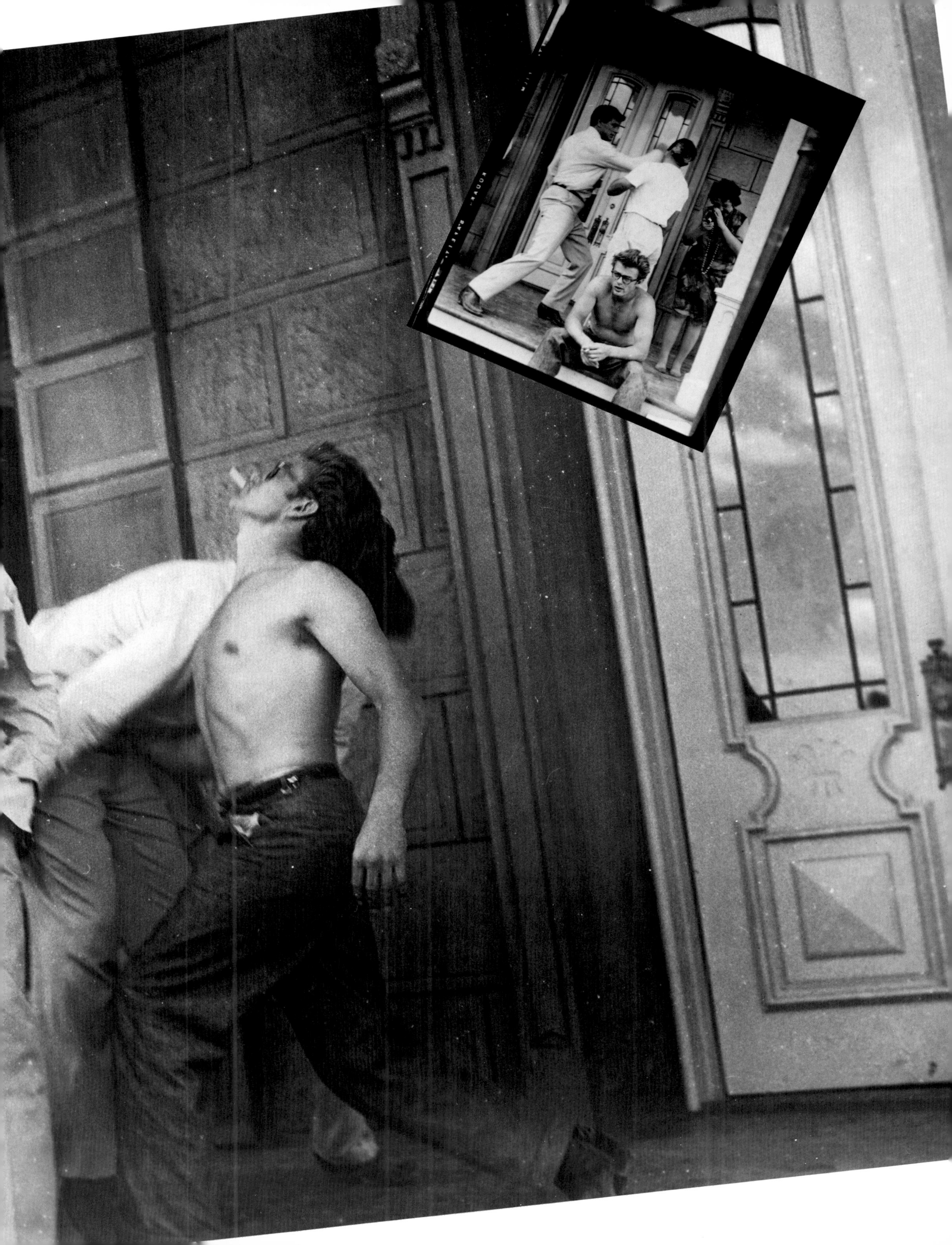

"James Dean has been checking in at Warner Bros. Studios at 6:30 each morning for his age makeup as Jett Rink in Giant, George Stevens' production of the Edna Ferber novel."

Warner Bros. Publicity Release; Ted Ashton: August, 1955

EXT. JETT'S SPECIAL BUILT CAR DAY 2" PROC. (REAR-SCREEN PROJECTION) MCS (MEDIUM CLOSE SHOT)

JETT AT WHEEL DRIVING CAR THRU OIL FIELDS L-R. HAS HAT ON—NO GLASSES.

CAMERA REPORT: GIANT; SCENE 277

"It was a great experience to work with Jimmy Dean. He was at once fully committed to the scene, entirely responsive to the other actor or actors, and yet a fierce competitor for first place."

Carroll Baker

James Dean passes the camera on his way to the dais in the Banquet Room of the "Conquistador hotel" as Guy Teague, Charles Watts and Ray Whitley obediently follow.

Bick Benedict squares off against a drunken Jett Rink in the liquor storage room of the "Conquistador Hotel."

"You ain't even worth hittin'—Jett, you want to know somethin' true? You're all washed up."
Bick Benedict
Giant

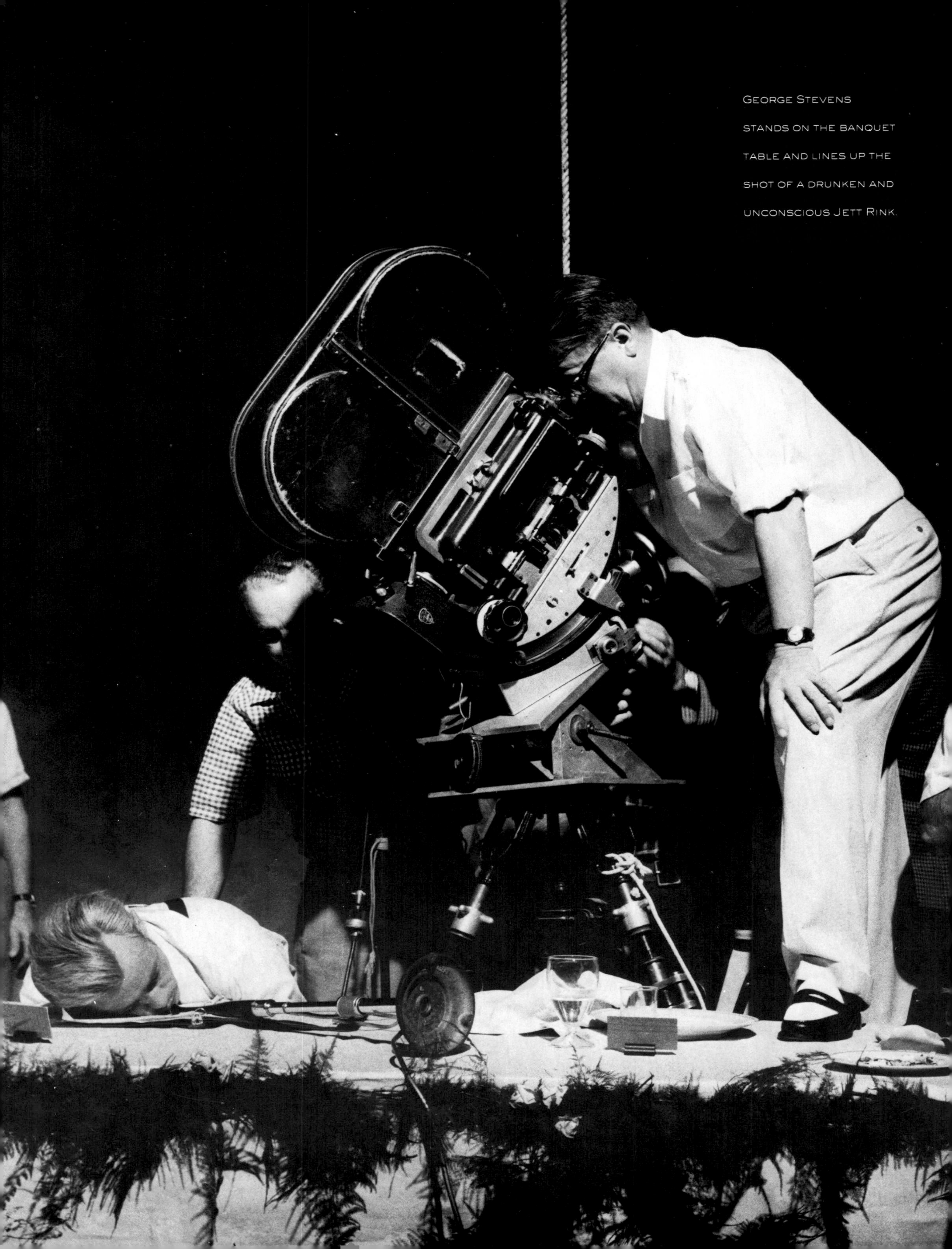

George Stevens stands on the banquet table and lines up the shot of a drunken and unconscious Jett Rink.

THE CAMERA CATCHES JETT RINK AWAKENING FROM HIS STUPOR, READY TO GIVE HIS SPEECH.

ROOM, ALONE ON
THE DAIS, FRAMED
BETWEEN TWO BOTTLES,
JETT RINK....

JR

....BEGINS HIS SPEECH.

"Sight of the week. James Dean twirling himself around like a whirling dervish on the set of <u>Giant</u> at Warner Bros. He does it to get dizzy going into his tipsy scenes in the picture."

Warner Bros. Publicity Release

Ted Ashton: 9/15/55

FORM 96 2500 SETS 5-54 SFP04608

DAILY PRODUCTION AND PROGRESS REPORT

W-C WIDE SCREEN

Day Saturday Date 10/1/55

Name of Production	"GIANT"	No.	403	Name of Director	GEORGE STEVENS
Number of Days Alloted	77	Started Production	5/19/55	Days Elapsed Since Starting	112
Status of Schedule:	34 DAYS BEHIND SCHED				

Estimated Finish Date: 8/22/55

Revised Finish Date (If Ahead or Behind):

Company Called	8:00A
Lng: Up.-Reh. 'til	11:58A
Started Shooting	11:58A
Lunch Called	12:32P
Time Started	1:32P
Dinner Called	
Time Started	
Time Finished	5:00P

SCRIPT REPORT

No. of Scenes Original Script	473
No. of Scenes Previously Taken	374
No. of Scenes Taken Today	0
Total Scenes Taken to Date	374
Balance to Be Taken	99
No. of Added Scenes Taken	16 + 0 = 16

Name of Set	Location	Finished?
INT. REATA MAIN HALL & LIBRARY - 02	STAGE 4	

CAST

S-Start W-Worked H-Held F-Finish R-Rehearse		Time Started	Time Finished	Slate No.	No. of Takes	Time of Ok Takes
ELIZABETH TAYLOR *	W	8:15A	5:00P	1695	1	
ROCK HUDSON	W	6:30A	5:00P	1696	2	
CHILL WILLS	W	6:30A	5:00P	1697	4	
TINA MENARD	W	7:30A	5:45P	1698	1	
EARL HOLLIMAN	WF	11:00A	4:45P			
FRAN BENNETT	WF	11:00A	4:45P			
DENNIS HOPPER	WF	11:00A	4:45P			
RAMON RAMIREZ	W	2:00P	5:00P			
Photog. Dble. Wkly:						
TERESA KNIGHT	W	7:30A	5:00P			

STAFF

		Time Started	Time Finished
Supervisor	Ginsberg		
Director	Stevens		
Dial. Dir.	Hinkle		
Unit Mgr.	Andre		
1st Asst.	Rickards		
2nd Asst.	Kilgore		
Extra Asst.			
Script Clerk	Freedle		
Cutter	Hornbeck		
Art Dir.	Leven		
Tech. Adv'r.			
CAMERMAN			
Head	Mellor		
2nd	Phillips		
Asst.	Mathews		
	Faubion		
Still Man	McCarty		
PROP MEN			
Head	Moor		

AUTOS

Stand by—

In Scenes—

Added Scenes Taken

...uler

5

PRODUCTION 34 DAYS BEHIND SCHEDULE

Remarks

* Note: ELIZABETH TAYLOR GRIEF STRICKEN REPORTED ON SET 11:45AM.

NOTE: Kindly indic... If any artist delays director st... ...riving later than time called, state rea...

Best Boy	
Grip	Harris
	Clair
Makeup	6 Men
Hair Dr.	2 Women
Wdrbe.	Vallejo
	Stutz

... Today	
To Date	
ORCHESTRA (W) (R)	
Total	
Called	
Dismissed	
Setups Today	4
Pages Today	1
Pages to Date	61-7/8

EXTRAS	ANIMALS	LUNCHES
10 Babies	1 Lamb 1 Calf	
STAND-INS	ANIMAL HANDLERS	AUTOS
		Stand by—

Script Scenes Taken

(Worked on Scenes 455 to end of script)

Added Scenes Taken

Call on Set | Finish on Set | Lunch | Dinner

Line up and Light
8:00-9:00AM
Wait for Miss Taylor who
was too upset from death
of James Dean, arrived to
studio at 11:45AM
Reh. 11:45-11:58AM
time includes setting of
animals 11:45-11:58AM.
A-1695 11:58-12:04PM
1 5'35" Print
Reload Camera take out
dolls set real childern
12:05-12:23PM
A-1696 12:23-12:30PM
1 Print
Line up and Light
12:30-12:32PM
LUNCH 12:32-1:32PM
Wait for Director
1:32-2:35PM
Reh. and set childern
2:35-2:40PM
A-1697 2:40-2:45PM
1 4'00" Print
Set Children and reload
2:45-2:59PM
Cont. shooting
A-1697 2:59-3:04PM
2 3'00" Print
Change Babies 3:05-3:12PM
Cont. shooting 3:12-3:18PM
3 3'00" Print
4 1'00" Print
Set two cameras 3:18-4:00PM
Light time included
Wait for Miss Taylor
4:00-4:50PM, time includes
redo of makeup.
Reh. 4:50-4:55PM
A-1698 4:55-5:00PM
1 5'50" Print
Miss Taylor unable to work
Co. Dismissed at 5:00PM

In order to keep their star happy and occupied, Warner Bros. and Elia Kazan, Nick Ray and George Stevens allowed James Dean to do something only a union studio photographer was allowed to do–shoot publicity photos during the making of *East of Eden, Rebel Without a Cause* and *Giant.*

The studio processed the film and the negatives and prints lingered behind with all the others that the Publicity Photo Department deemed unnecessary for the general promotion of the movies. They too ended up in the WB Archives at USC, mixed in with all the other negs and prints from the three films.

But something about these photos made them stand out. At first, it was their utterly unprofessional quality...odd angles often coupled with murky lighting. "What the hell are these?" was our first thought when Keith and I started our search through the material.

Then the realization hit. These were the photos Dean was allowed to take of his fellow actors–his directors–his girlfriend. Here is Pier Angeli–too beautiful for words–at her makeup table for *The Silver Chalice.* There is Raymond Massey on his 'death bed' as Adam Trask...and Barbara Baxley as his nurse...and there's Julie Harris vamping for the camera...and Elia Kazan mugging...and Nick Ray glowering. Natalie Wood is there, too...and even some unnamed microphone boom men...all seen through the eye of James Dean. Here, then, is JAMES DEAN–BEHIND THE CAMERA.

BEHIND THE CAMERA

2
6

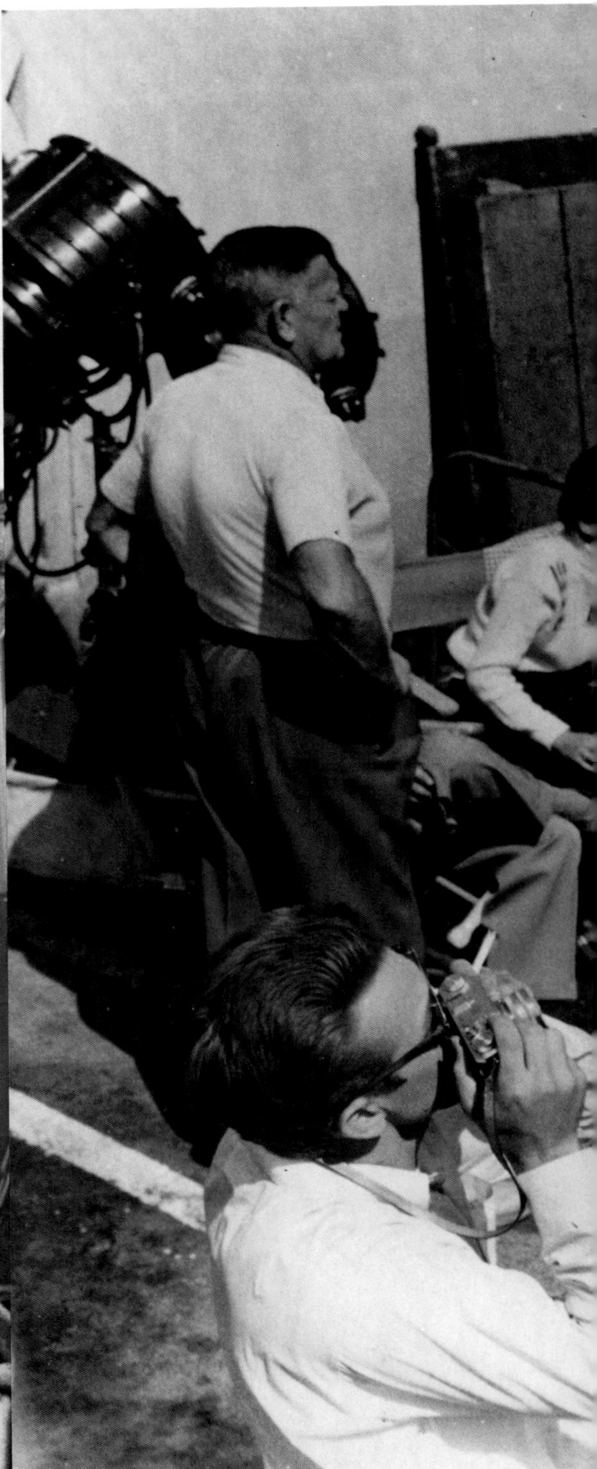

Rebel Without a Cause, 1955

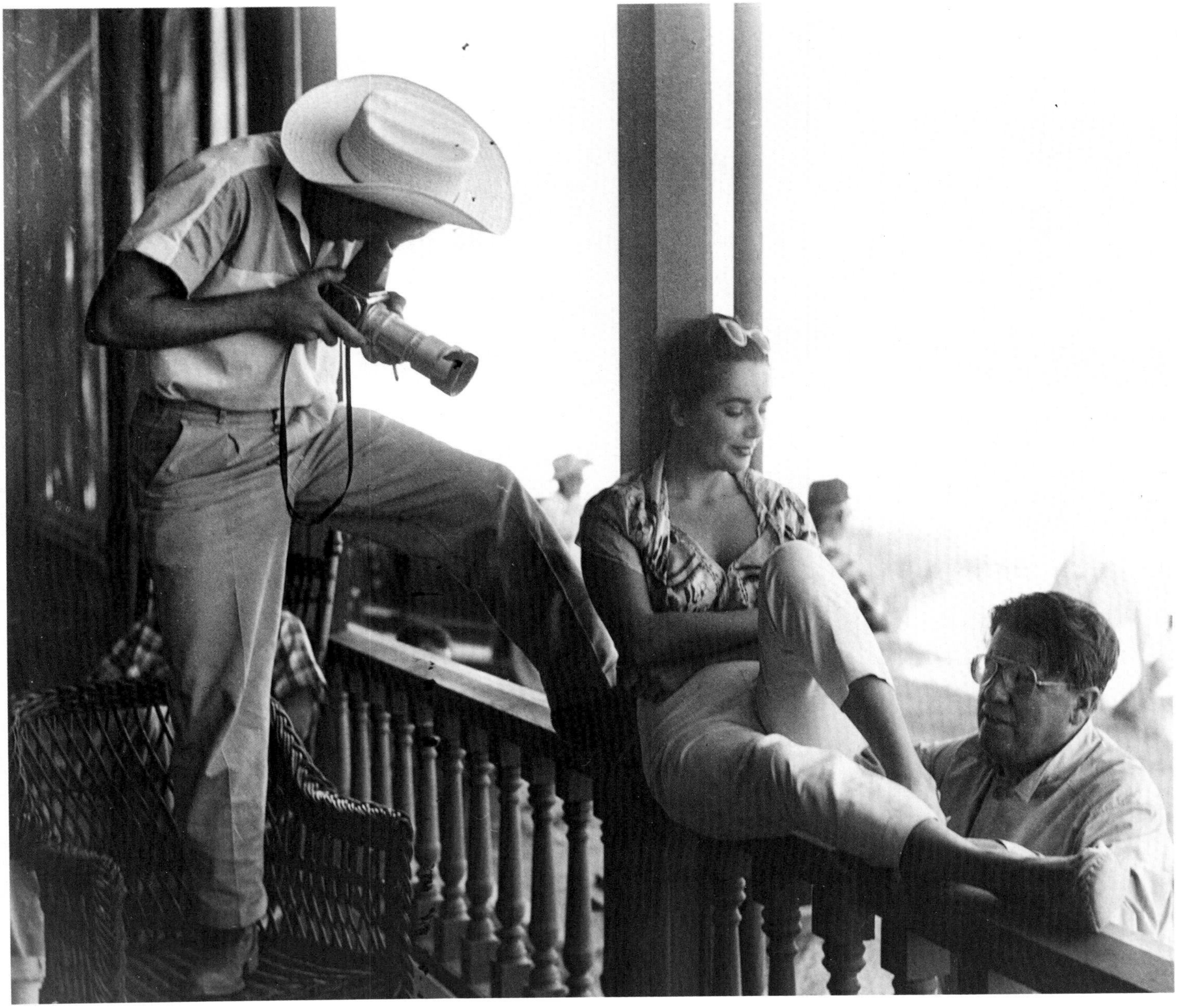

Giant, 1955

Pier Angeli, 1954

SAFETY FILM
KODAK SAFETY FILM

Elia Kazan and Julie Harris, 1954

Julie Harris, 1954

BARBARA BAXLEY, 1954

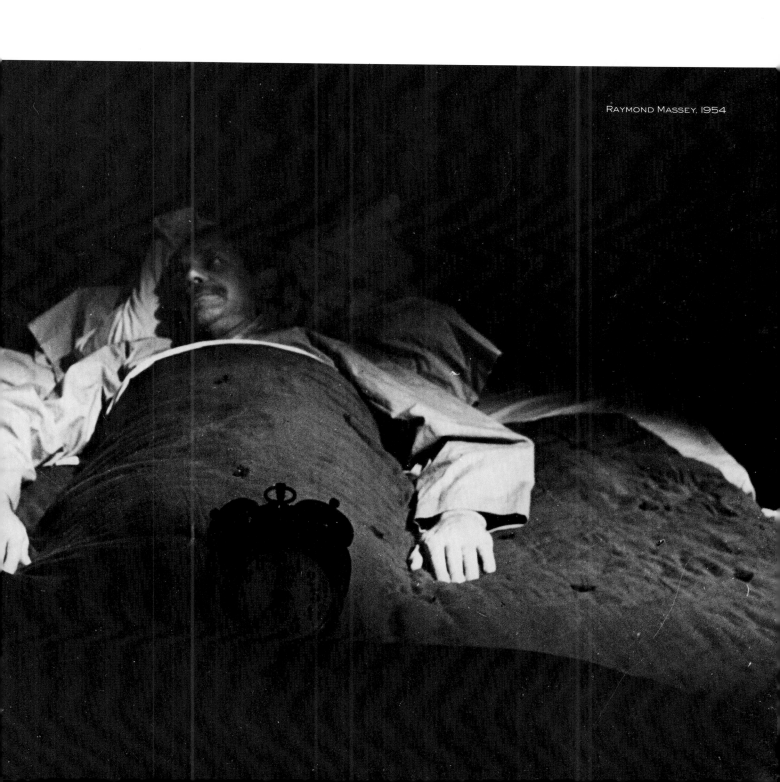

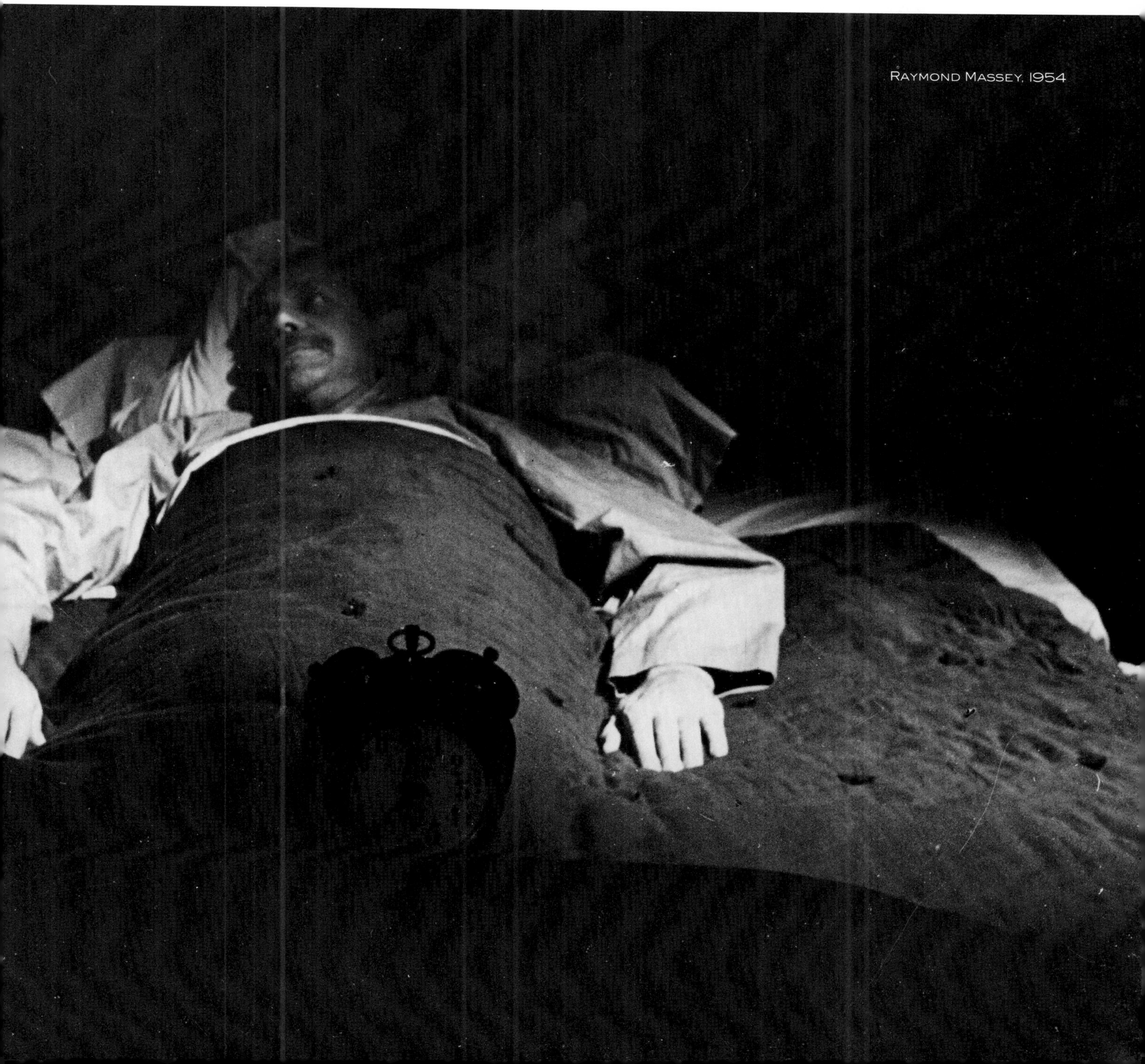
RAYMOND MASSEY, 1954

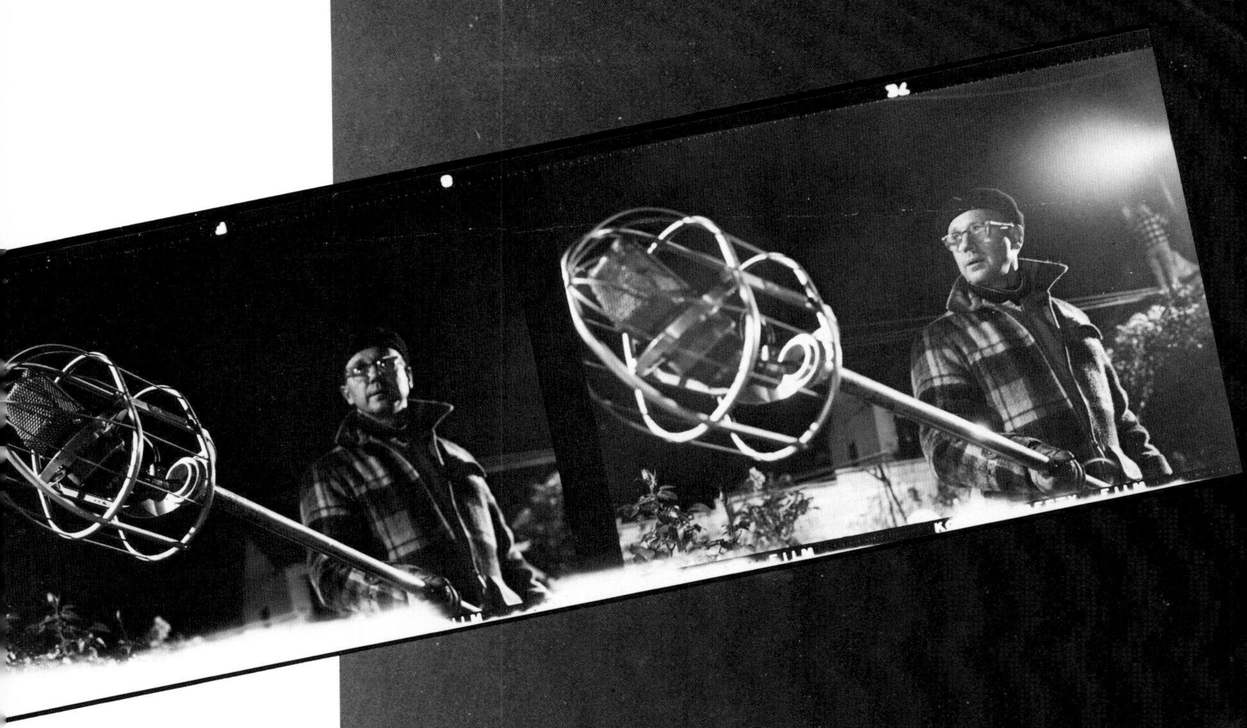

—Holding boom mike

Natalie Wood.

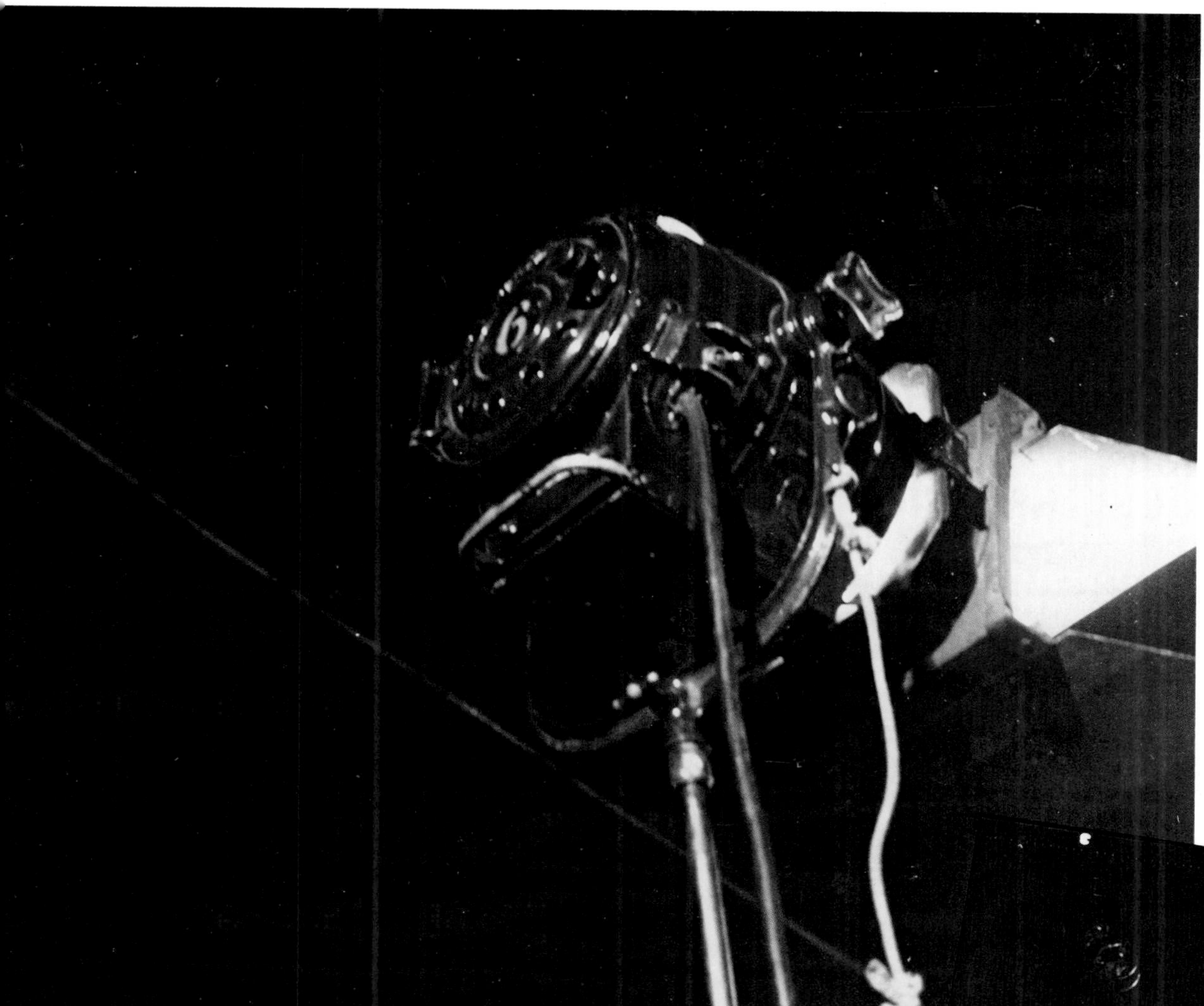

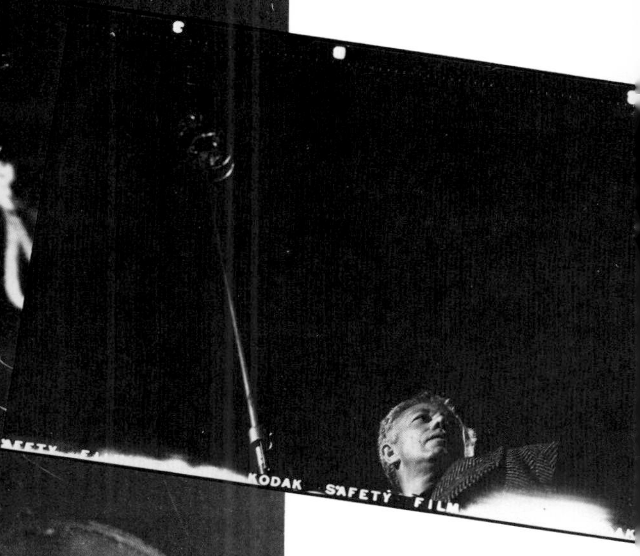

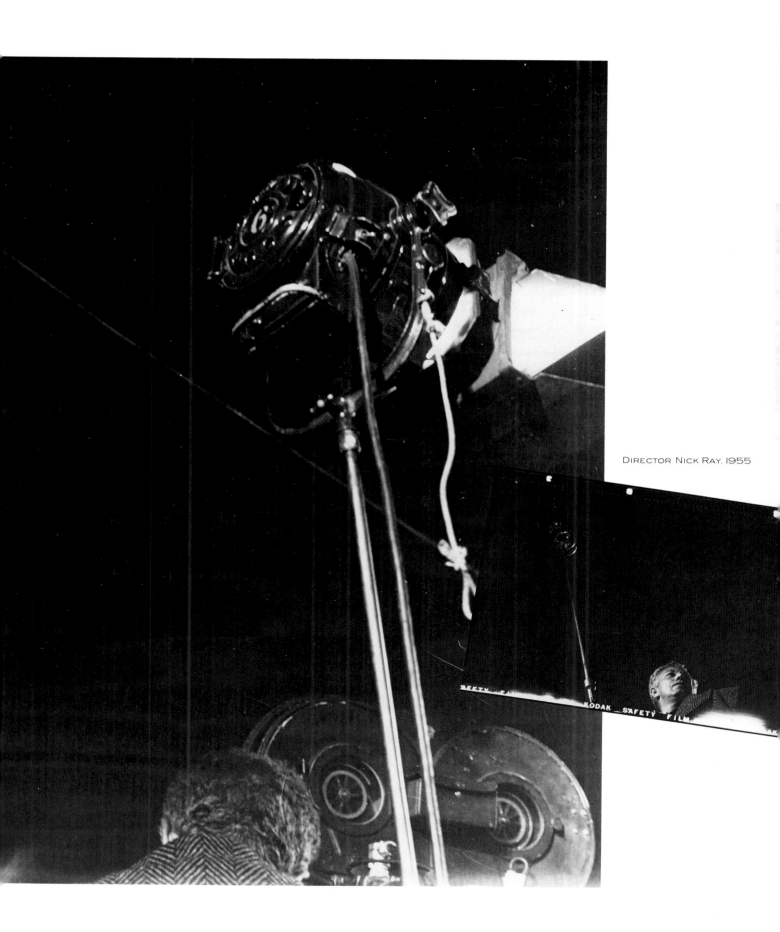

Director Nick Ray, 1955

FLOYD MCCARTY'S HOTEL ROOM, MARFA, TEXAS, 1955

Special Dedication

This book is gratefully dedicated to the still photographers of East of Eden, Rebel Without a Cause and Giant: Jack Albin, Bert Longworth, Floyd McCarty, Gjon Mili, Jack Woods, Mac Julian, Pat Clark and Gene Kornmann. It is through their eyes and their photographs that the image and legend of James Dean first began and which has continued to capture millions upon millions of fans around the world in the thirty-five years since he made his last film....

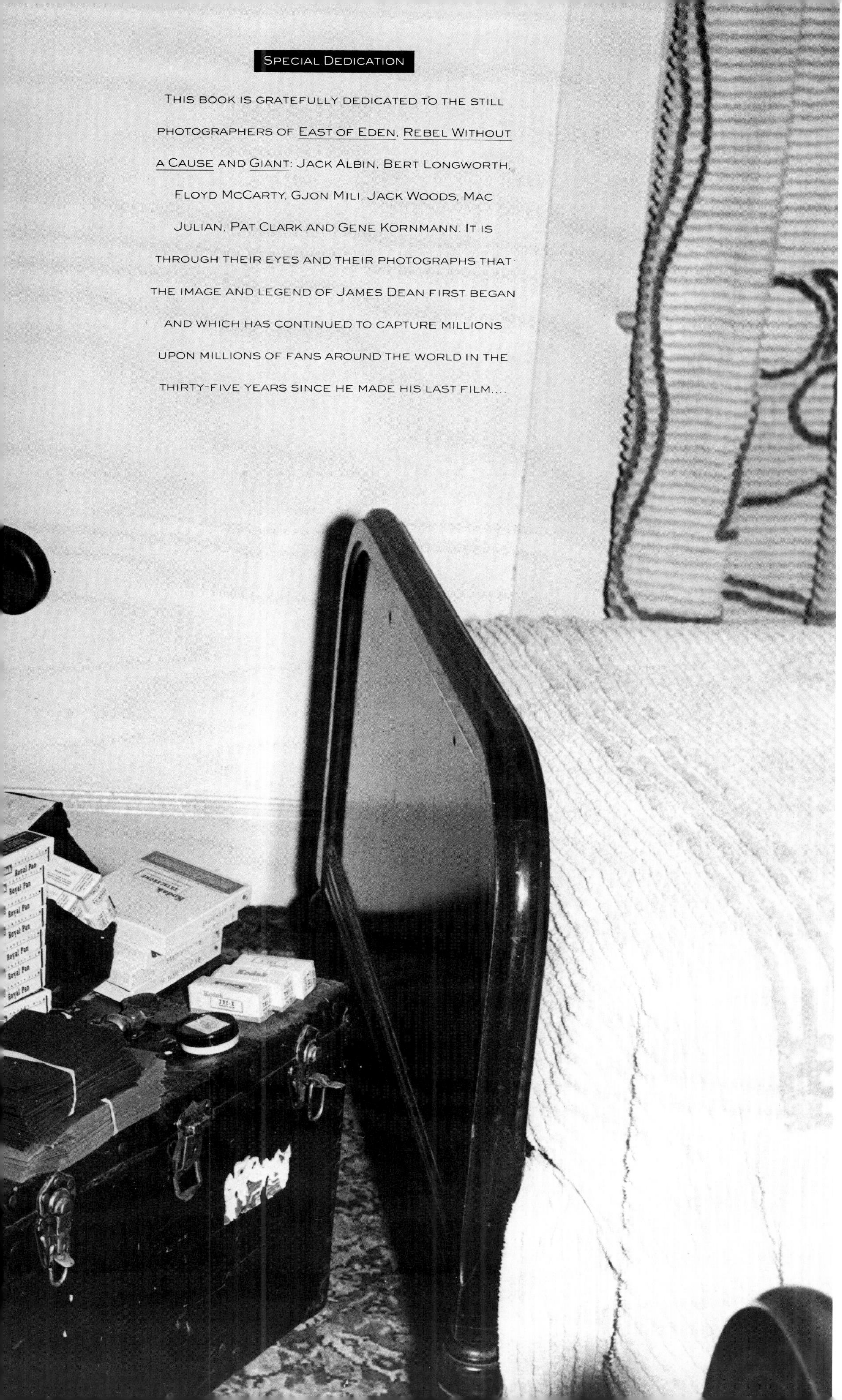

EPILOGUE

"*On* Friday, September 30, around six o'clock, Elizabeth, Rock and I and a small group were watching the rushes. George Stevens was behind us at his desk by the controls. The projection room was dark. The phone rang. The soundtrack screamed to a halt. The picture froze. The lights shot up. We turned and looked at George. The phone dangled in his hand. He was white and motionless. Death was present in that room. Slowly and with great effort, his voice coming from a long and distant tunnel, George said, " 'There's been a car crash. Jimmy Dean has been killed.' I went numb."

CARROLL BAKER

HEDDA HOPPER FILE ON WB STATIONERY

Oct. 5, 1955

Miss Hedda Hopper
6331 Hollywood Blvd.
Hollywood, Calif.

Dear Miss Hopper:

I'm very grateful to you for the beautiful eulogy in your column about Jimmy Dean.

I was Mr. Kazan's secretary on EAST OF EDEN and knew (and understood) Jimmy from that moment on. You're right–this boy had a lot of love to give, but perhaps was afraid of being rejected, like so many sensitive people. The birthday scene in EAST OF EDEN, which was almost unbearable to watch, must have been easy for Jimmy to do. I'll always be haunted by that terrible sob that seemed to come from his soul.

It's too bad that people judge that first deceiving, unimportant layer instead of trying to understand sensitive people–there's a lot of good stuff underneath! Toothy, insincere smiles and glad hands are a dime a dozen.

Thank you again–very much.

Sincerely,

Rhea Burakoff

1830 N. Cherokee
Hollywood 28, Calif.

HENRY GINSBERG COLLECTION

Thursday October 6

Dear John–

The passing of James Dean was indeed very tragic. He had a magnificent career ahead of him. He had completed his role in our picture two weeks before the accident, hence there was nothing further that he was required to do for us. He gave a great performance in GIANT and his ageing from the early 20's to about 50 years is most realistic and convincing. The consensus of opinion personality and may develop into something of a legend. Considering that he was a character actor, the feeling is that his appearance in films will not be affected at all, if anything there may be greater anxiety on the part of the public to see him. It must be borne in mind that he only made one picture thus far released which, as you know, is EAST OF EDEN, and he reached stardom overnight. Warners have another picture unreleased–REBEL WITHOUT A CAUSE. Although I have not seen it, I am told that it is only fair, however, his performance is most outstanding. This picture will be released sometime in November and this may be a guide somewhat to public reaction. Our picture GIANT is naturally protected by other star personalities and we probably will not release our picture for another year. Of course the thinking that I am giving you is of today and it is difficult to say what will happen a year hence.

I am leaving here in the morning for Fairmont, Indiana to attend Dean's funeral services and I will return to the coast on Sunday.

My love and best to you,

Dad

HEDDA HOPPER COLLECTION

From Wed. Oct. 5, 1955 Column

"I'm still reeling from the sudden death of Jimmy Dean, one of the greatest acting talents I've ever known. He was a tragic figure. So few understood him. He was reaching out for love and understanding, but got so little. His greatest ambition was to play Hamlet on Broadway. Said he, "It should be done only by a young man." The thing that he loved the most was the thing that killed him–his racing car. He carried with him in death the St. Christopher medal Pier Angeli gave him while he was making "EAST OF EDEN." He was like quicksilver. He had a sure instinct for drama. He was like the parched earth longing for the rain. Only a few days ago a friend of mine met him in a pet hospital. He had brought a kitten for an innoculation and the loving care he was giving it was beautiful to look upon. It will be a long time before we see his like again. I loved the boy and always will."

ACKNOWLEDGMENTS

To the following people, without whose help, inspiration and support, this book would not exist....
Mr. Bernard Kurman: Rights Unlimited Agency

Warner Bros. Inc.: Luana Chambers, Dan Romanelli, Patricia Brown, Marshall Silverman, Judy Singer, Jeremy Williams, John Schulman, Betty Buckley, Irene Slade, Paula Reno, Jackie Kelly, Wendy Abbott.

USC: Herbert Farmer, Anne Schlosser, Ned Constock, Victoria Steele, Carolyn Harrison, Robert Knutson.

UCLA: Brigitte Kueppers, Raymond Soto, David Zeidberg, James Davis.

Producers Photo Lab: Knight Harris, Clark Harris, Lee Lawrence, Scott Libolt, Craig Bright, Herayr Nazarian.

Margaret Herrick Library, Academy of Motion Picture Arts & Sciences: Sam Gill, Stacey Endres, Howard Prouty, Linda Mehr.

Birch Lane Press: Hillel Black, Sandy Richardson, Gail Kinn, Steven Schragis, Bruce Bender, Steven Brower, Jessica Black, Ben Petrone, Fern Edison.

Book Castle of Burbank, California: Paul Hunt, Steve Edrington.

The entire staff of Movie World in Burbank, California.

Dennis Hopper, John Waxman, Sid Avery, Bill Zavatsky, Faith McNulty, Douglas M. Spruance, James Erlandson, Natasha Arnoldi, Robin Berg, the Henry Ginsberg Family.

To Wyatt and Jane Adams and Harry and Rose Burns who gave us the money for the tickets and put the boxes of popcorn into our hands... our parents, who hooked us on the movies forever.

And especially to Char Adams and Joan Perkal for their love and support through the years it has taken this book to reach this moment and for allowing us and the book to spill over into the living rooms of their lives.

ACKNOWLEDGMENTS FOR BOOK QUOTES

Grateful acknowledgement is given to the following publishers for their permission to reprint the excerpts included in this book.

Backus, Jim. *Rocks On the Roof.* New York: G.P. Putnam Sons, 1958

Baker, Carroll. *Baby Doll–An Autobiography.* New York: Arbor House, 1983

Chekmayan, Ara. *Forever James Dean.* A Chelsea Communications Production, 1988

Hopper, Hedda. *The Whole Truth and Nothing But.* New York: Doubleday, 1963

Kazan, Elia. *A Life.* New York: Alfred A. Knopf, 1988

Massey, Raymond. *A Hundred Different Lives.* Boston: Little, Brown and Company, 1979

McCambridge, Mercedes. *The Quality of Mercy.* Times Books. New York, 1981

Sheinwald, Patricia Fox. *Too Young to Die.* Baltimore: Ottenheimer Publishing, Inc., 1979

EAST OF EDEN

Warner Bros. (Released March 1955)

Produced and directed by Elia Kazan; Screenplay by Paul Osborn; Based on the novel by John Steinbeck; Cinematography, Ted McCord; Art direction, James Basevi and Malcolm Bert, Musical direction, Leonard Rosenman; Editor, Owen Marks. CinemaScope and WarnerColor. 115 minutes

James Dean (Cal Trask); Julie Harris (Abra); Raymond Massey (Adam Trask); Burl Ives (Sam); Jo Van Fleet (Kate); Richard Davalos (Aron Trask); Albert Dekker (Will); Lois Smith (Anne); Harold Gordon (Mr. Albrecht); Richard Garrick (Dr. Edwards); Timothy Carey (Joe); Nick Dennis (Rantini); Lonnie Chapman (Roy); Barbara Baxley (Nurse); Bette Treadville (Madame); Tex Mooney (Bartender); Harry Cording (Bartender); Loretta Rush (Card Dealer); Bill Phillips (Coalman); Mario Siletti (Piscora); Jonathan Haze (Piscora's Son); Jack Carr, Effie Laird, Wheaton Chambers, Ed Clark, Al Ferguson, Franklyn Farnum, Rose Plummer (Carnival People); John George (Photographer); Earle Hodgins (Shooting Gallery Attendant); C. Ramsey Hill (English Officer); Edward McNally (Soldier)

(James Dean was nominated for an Academy Award as Best Actor)

REBEL WITHOUT A CAUSE

Warner Bros. (Released October 1955)

Produced by David Weisbart; Directed by Nicholas Ray; Screenplay by Stewart Stern; Based on Irving Shulman's adaptation of a story by Nicholas Ray; Cinematography, Ernest Haller; Art direction, Malcolm Bert; Costumes, Moss Mabry; Musical direction, Leonard Rosenman; Editor, William Ziegler. CinemaScope and WarnerColor. 111 minutes.

James Dean (Jim); Natalie Wood (Judy); Sal Mineo (Plato); Jim Backus (Jim's Father); Ann Doran (Jim's Mother); Corey Allen (Buzz); William Hopper (Judy's Father); Rochelle Hudson (Judy's Mother); Virginia Brissac (Jim's Grandma); Nick Adams (Moose); Jack Simmons (Cookie); Dennis Hopper (Goon); Marietta Canty (Plato's Maid); Jack Grinnage (Chick); Beverly Long (Helen); Steffi Sidney (Mil); Frank Mazzola (Crunch); Tom Bernard (Harry); Clifford Morris (Cliff); Ian Wolfe (Lecturer); Edward Platt (Ray); Robert Foulk (Gene); Jimmy Baird (Beau); Dick Wessel (Guide); Nelson Leigh (Sergeant); Dorothy Abbott (Nurse); Louise Lane (Woman Officer); House Peters (Officer); Gus Schilling (Attendant); Bruce Noonan (Monitor); Almira Sessions (Old Lady Teacher); Peter Miller (Hoodlum); Paul Bryar (Desk Sergeant); Paul Birch (Police Chief); Robert B. Williams (Moose's Father); David McMahon (Crunch's Father)

GIANT

Warner Bros. (Released October 1956)

Produced by George Stevens and Henry Ginsberg; Directed by George Stevens; Screenplay by Fred Guiol and Ivan Moffat; Based on the novel by Edna Ferber; Cinematography, William C. Mellor; Production designer, Boris Leven; Costumes, Marjorie Best and Moss Mabry; Musical score, Dimitri Tiomkin; Song "There's Never Been Anyone Else But You" by Dimitri Tiomkin and Paul Francis Webster; Editor, William Hornbeck. WarnerColor. 198 minutes

Elizabeth Taylor (Leslie Lynnton Benedict); Rock Hudson (Bick Benedict); James Dean (Jett Rink); Carroll Baker (Luz Benedict II); Jane Withers (Vashti Snythe); Chill Wills (Uncle Bawley); Mercedes McCambridge (Luz Benedict); Sal Mineo (Angel Obregon III); Dennis Hopper (Jordan Benedict III); Judith Evelyn (Mrs. Horace Lynnton); Paul Fix (Dr. Horace Lynnton); Rodney Taylor (Sir David Karfrey); Earl Holliman (Bob Dace); Robert Nichols (Pinky Snythe); Alexander Scourby (Old Polo); Fran Bennett (Judy Benedict); Charles Watts (Whiteside); Elsa Cardenas (Juana); Carolyn Craig (Lacey Lynnton); Monte Hale (Bale Clinch); Mary Ann Edwards (Adarene Clinch); Sheb Wooley (Gabe Target); Victor Millan (Angel Obregon I): Mickey Simpson (Sarge); Pilar del Rey (Mrs. Obregon); Maurice Jara (Dr. Guerra); Noreen Nash (Lona Lane); Napoleon Whiting (Swazey); Tina Menard (Lupe); Ray Whitley (Watts); Felipe Turich (Gomez); Francisco Villalobos (Mexican Priest); Ana Maria Majalca (Petra); Guy Teague (Harper); Nativadid Vacio (Eusebio); Max Terhune (Dr. Walker); Ray Bennett (Dr. Borneholm); Barbara Barrie (Mary Lou Decker); George Dunne (Verne Decker); Slim Talbot (Clay Hodgins); Tex Driscoll (Clay Hodgins, Sr.); Juney Ellis (Essie Lou Hodgins)

(James Dean was nominated for an Academy Award as Best Actor)